Raccoon
Theology

and other musings from a
mountain newspaper columnist

Earl C. Davis

Rocky Comfort Press

Preface

For the past several years I have had the pleasure of looking out over the Yadkin Valley, perched far above the towns of Lenoir and Morganton and Hickory. Sandwiched between mountains with picturesque names like Winding Stair is Happy Valley and churches with names like *Just a Closer Walk Baptist Church.*

The privilege of serving some of the churches "down the mountain" from Blowing Rock where my wife, Pegeen, and I live has been a delight. In one of those churches I met the editor of the Lenoir *News-Topic* and was invited to contribute a week-end column in the area of religion. For several years now I have enjoyed quietly reflecting on such things as raccoon theology, Christ without a bucket, and listening to Tweetsie blowing just over the hill. In these pages are found some of those musings which have brought kind comments from friends "down the mountain."

It seemed best to put these thoughts under several categories, such as *Animal (and birds and bees) Theology, A Pastor's Pilgrimage, Thoughts on Special Days, Reflection on Biblical Texts,* and *Modern Parables.* Some of the columns reflect certain churches in which I was interim pastor at the time, and other columns reflect current events at the time.

If you are provided once again with a chuckle, or a moment of reflection on a truth, or an fresh insight, I am well repaid.

Dedicated in love

to the one who has been by my side in pastorates in Virginia, Kentucky, Florida, Georgia, Tennessee and now in our ninth interim pastorate in North Carolina.
As one dear friend put it succinctly upon our retirement: It will be hard to replace you, but impossible to replace Pegeen!

Contents

Chapter One

Animal (and Birds and Bees) Theology

Raccoon Theology

Preachers have odd friends—when they have friends at all! I remember how, in my first pastorate after seminary, I befriended a delinquent church member who operated a liquor store. I failed to realize how small our town was, and how rapidly gossip traveled! I had been visiting the liquor store owner at his establishment for a few weeks when another church member took me aside and shared the facts of life. The liquor store owner, he said, really did appreciate my visits, and was glad I did not shun him—but my friendship was about to put him out of business! Nobody wanted to have the Baptist preacher drop by the liquor store when they might be in there purchasing a little medicinal aid!

But I met one of my oddest friends on a visit to New England some years ago. While enjoying the foliage one October we came across a woodworking shop where the artist created wonderfully carved animals in human poses. I was quite taken by a carved raccoon, standing with one hand in his overall pocket and the other holding up a sign, which could be changed to say whatever you wished. I liked the little guy and bought him. When folks visit our home, he usually stands patiently at the front door with a sign welcoming them. He gets a lot of comments, and I think everybody needs a friend or two like him— you know, friends who lead folks to ask you, "Where'd you get that friend?" After all, they asked Jesus that, too. See John 18:19.

Not long ago I had been at a conference all day, and it was close to dusk when I got home. "I'm glad you got home before dark," said my wife. "Come look—somebody's eating our house!" She took me outside, and we could see that in at least three places, one of them about 8 feet long, something—or somebody—had indeed been eating the bottom row of roof shingles, just above the gutter. At first I couldn't believe it, but there it was—our roof was being eaten away!

It's funny how a sight like holes eaten in your roof can sharpen your memory. We remembered the pitty-pat of tiny feet on the roof over our bedroom. And then there was the time we saw a cat jump from the fence onto our roof and run along it. (Your cats aren't acrobats?) It seemed odd to me, too. But, if we haven't seen any raccoons in the years we have lived in this house, would this be raccoons? Or what about squirrels— they're famous for eating their way into attics and down chimneys.

And then the thought crept in: you don't suppose my little overall-wearing, sign totin' raccoon friend is cavorting around after hours . . . or is he? Maybe we're being invaded by a gang of his friends. Nah; this is an orderly world where wooden raccoons don't become real ones . . . or do they? After all, C. S. Lewis has a wonderful essay in which he says that the essence of Christianity is that we are all little toy soldiers, and there is a rumour going around that someday we're going to come alive.

It was all-out war. I borrowed two "catch 'em alive" traps from a church member and proceeded on the assumption that I was after squirrels, cats, opposums or some other terrifying beast. Careful examination of various bait options revealed that sardines smelled bad enough to do the job. So, flashlight in hand, I sloshed through a drizzle on the first night to set the traps on the ground near one of the "destruction areas" of the roof.

Mama in her kerchief, and I in my cap, had just settled down for the night when we heard the sound of tiny feet on the roof. A dash to the window with flashlight in hand revealed a bare trap. Another half-hour brought the sound of a sardine tin rattling against the wire cage (hollering for more, I reckoned as I jumped out of bed). Again the flashlight, and this time the yard floodlights were also turned on—"stand still, we've got you covered, you varmint!" And would you believe it; there he was, the cookie monster of our roof, glaring balefully at me from beyond his mask. Ringed tail and Lone Ranger mask, sans overalls, there he stood—a first cousin of my sign-totin' wooden raccoon friend.

The next question from my wife: What to do with this nocturnal roof-hopping, shingle-eating bandit? Kill him? Give him to someone who will turn him into stew? Or take him several miles away and turn him loose? Without really thinking it through, I responded: "For the sake of the raccoon on the front porch, I'm going to turn him loose!" And then it hit me. It may be raccoon theology, but it has the ring of Gospel truth: "Because of *that* one—let *this* one go free." And so I carried that little bandit far away and let him go . . .

For the sake of the one who died on the cross, there is the possibility of all us sinners going free. But unlike my masked friend, it takes repentance on our part.

Be Ye Like Geese

Until I retired (?) and moved to *Rocky Comfort*, our place on the Blue Ridge, I was a pastor for 25 years in Memphis, Tennessee. As pastor for 18 years of the First Baptist Church in Memphis and then for six years the founding pastor of Trinity Baptist Church, I managed to stay busy. But I still found time for duck and goose hunting. One memorable goose hunting trip was to Monkey's Eyebrow, Kentucky, just over the state line. I bagged two geese, traded them in at the packing plant for two dressed and frozen geese, and when I came home with those frozen geese I had a hard time convincing my wife I actually killed geese that day. My best effort at convincing her was to say that I did kill those very geese, and because they were flying so high when I shot them, during the fall they were skinned, dressed and frozen. I'm not sure she bought it! But goose hunting gives you time while sitting in the blind to think about goose theology. Here are some goose theology points every pastor and every church member should ponder.

Fact 1: As each goose in a flying gaggle flaps its wings, it creates an "uplift" for the birds that follow. By flying in a "V" formation, the whole flock adds 71% greater flying range than if each bird flew alone. Lesson: People who share a common direction and sense of community can get where they are going quicker and easier because they are traveling on the thrust of one another. Now this is based on all the geese flying. I don't know what happens when some of the geese decide to quit flapping and coast on the efforts of the others. But I do know bad things happen in church when 20% of the folks do 80% of the work and give 80% of the offerings.

Fact 2: When a goose falls out of formation, it suddenly feels the drag and resistance of flying alone. It quickly moves back into the formation to take advantage of the lifting power of the bird immediately in front of it. Lesson: if we have as much sense as geese, we will stay in formation with those headed where we want to go. When we are willing to accept their help and give our help to others, we get a better understanding of the Biblical concept of church and of being a pilgrim heading for a certain destination.

Fact 3: When the lead goose tires, it rotates back in the formation and another goose flies to the point position. Lesson: It pays to take turns doing the hard tasks and sharing the leadership. As with geese, people are interdependent on each other's skills, capabilities and unique arrangements of gifts, talents or resources. God gives each Christian at least one spiritual gift to build up the church. If we do not use our spiritual gifts, the church suffers.

Fact 4: The geese flying in formation honk to encourage those up front to keep up their speed. Lesson: We need to make sure our honking is encouraging. In groups where there is encouragement, the production is much, much greater. The power of encouragement (to stand by one's heart or core values and encourage the heart and core of others) is the quality of honking we seek. A word to the wise: studies show it takes 13 positive comments to offset one negative comment. When did you last say an encouraging word to your pastor?

Fact 5: When a goose gets sick, wounded or shot down, two geese drop out of formation and follow it down to help protect it. They stay with it until it dies or it is able to fly again. Then, they launch out with another formation or catch up with the flock. Lesson: If we have as much sense as geese, we will stay by each other in difficult times as well as when we are strong. Odd, isn't it, that in the church of all places, we shun those who are crippled by sin. Jesus didn't. Mighty good theology from a goose. File these thoughts under Galatians 6:1,2 and Ephesians 4:2,3; 5:21.

The Wiley Trout

The payoff came last weekend. My neighbor, who loves long dog walks but didn't know one end of a fly rod from the other (that's the way it is with those CIA types), decided last summer to give in to my entreaties and let me teach him to fly fish. Not that it was a "do as I do" thing; it was more a "ignore how I do it, and do as I say" thing.

After he got over the idea of the hook hurting the fish's jaw, he advanced to the point of making an occasional passable cast as last summer wound down. Last fall, he bought a pair of waders. A big leap of faith, that was. So, last Friday I suggested he try out his new waders in my favorite trout hangout (no, I won't tell where that is).

We started at the "smokehouse", the hole on the creek that usually rewards a decent cast with a strike or two, if not a fish. I got a nice brown trout, 12-14 inches or so (put more weight on the "or so"). Then lost him after netting him, between the net and the creel! We ambled on down the stream, and the patron saint of fly fishermen decided to smile on us. One side of the creek is heavily rocked, with the current moving down that side. We took turns casting into those enchanted waters, and were rewarded with nine more trout ranging from 8 to 14 inches. One nice trout hit the wooly booger I was casting four times without getting hooked! But there's nothing quite like the flash of a trout as he goes for a dry fly floating by!

A nice rainbow surfaced and splashed some 15 yards down the creek; my neighbor made a lucky cast and apparently put the lure in the fish's mouth! That was a nice trout! It was time to leave the stream, but what is the call of supper compared to trout feeding on the surface at sunset? I found eager reception for wooly boogers, dry flies and even nymphs. I'm not sure what turned the fish on, but it was a perfect couple of hours for fly fishermen.

The only fly in the ointment was that my neighbor caught the biggest, a 14 inch brown that really lived up to his name. As I told my neighbor, "It doesn't get much better for a fly fisherman than this." I think, for the first time, he actually understood the pull of fly fishing for me.

Naturally, thinking back on that golden afternoon, I got to thinking how those trout must have been Baptist trout. You see, I went back on Tuesday morning before breakfast. Did I hook a big one at the "smokehouse?" Not on your tintype. In fact, in an hour of retracing the fantastic route of four days earlier, I got only one little tap on the lure. Now, that's the way I have always found Baptists to be. You can't count on them following the rules, or acting the same way twice.

Baptists are individualistic and independent. We pride ourselves on thinking for ourselves. And just when the pastor thinks he's got the dynamics of a congregation figured out—like I thought I had those trout figured out after the magic afternoon—they fool him. This business of fishing for men is not as simple as it appears!

Well, back to my fish story. On Tuesday night, we invited my neighbor and his wife over for a fish dinner. It was a perfect ending to the fish story—my neighbor has the fishing bug, I think; and we enjoyed the trout for dinner. Here's how I fixed those trout: clean them, split or fillet them, and then first dip them in an egg dip. Then, dip them, flesh side down, in a coating of seasoned meal and flour and butter and chopped pecans. Then, on your old homemade gas grill—it's like a blowtorch on legs!—saute them daddies for about 2 minutes on each side, and you're ready for some good eating.

Oh, yeah—don't forget the hushpuppies.

A Bit of Dog Theology

I think you've met our collie, Princess, who is an Old Testament dog. Then there's her playmate, Jasper, who belongs to my neighbor and is a New Testament dog. Jasper lives to retrieve sticks you throw. He's a rather silly sight, crouching some 50 feet ahead on the path, every muscle straining entirely oblivious to everything else, and waiting for the blessed pitch of the stick into the air towards him. His is the joy of doing what he is designed to do—retrieve, whether it is a stick or a duck or a quail. Now, if he's fast and lucky, he can get to the stick without being herded off to the side by Princess. Because she is simply doing what she is designed to do, and that is to herd things—other dogs, sheep, or whatever is out there and moving!

Contrary to New Testament Jasper, Princess is an Old Testament dog, and I'll tell you why. I put up an electronic, invisible barrier to mark out our yard. Princess has a collar which will first beep, and then give her a shock if she goes past the invisible boundary. She's learned that lesson so well that she will not, under any circumstances, go out of our driveway beyond the boundary. Not even if I take the collar off. Not even if I beg and plead with her. Not even bribery with mmm-mm-m tasty dog biscuits will work. That's one more dumb dog! But, I should give her credit for being a most obedient, loving dog.

But can you imagine a guy having to take her collar off, opening the trunk of his SUV, having her jump in, then driving 100 feet away to the end of the drive and parking, and then letting her out? That's what I have to do in order to get her to go for a walk. I must take her in the car past the boundary line, then let her out.

Well, that became the pattern this fall and winter. Load Princess up, drive past the boundary and park. Then she will happily gallop down the road to our neighbor's house. By the way, have you ever noticed your collie loping, or running? They run weird, or at least this one does. Anyhow, when we rendezvous with my neighbor and Jasper walking toward our house, there is a great welcome scene. The two dogs first race wildly around in great circles before quieting down for the walk. The other day they came barreling by us in the wild chase, and actually knocked my neighbor down. Now, being a former "spook" he should be smarter than to get in the way of 175 pounds of flying dogs! But he wasn't, and they laid him out! It has turned out to be something like a sprained knee with all kinds of stressed tendons. Crutches for the first couple of weeks, then hobbling around for another month or so. Which means that now every morning I load Princess up, drive over to the neighbor's house, and take both dogs out for the traditional morning walk.

Why am I telling you all this? Well, it strikes me that some folks are Old Testament believers, like Princess, focussing more on the "don'ts" of religion than on the joys. Obedience is designed to bring joy and delight into life; that's the point of the Bible, to bring us back to our rightful relationship with God. Only through obeying God's rules can we reach our potential. But we are not to be obsessed with the negative, like the old Puritans, of whom it is said they were always afraid somebody, somewhere, was having fun! They were herders like Princess, never forgetting the stern rules themselves, and trying to stop others from having fun by retrieving the stick!

Now some folks are like Jasper, so caught up in the excitement, the joy of fulfilling his calling to retrieve, that they don't use all their mind! I've seen lots of Christians who seemed to wear blinders about the world in which they live. They are afraid the Bible will be discredited; that God will be deposed, etc. etc. The Bible is quite capable of defending itself, thank you. And God certainly doesn't depend on my help or yours to run this world! Our purpose is to walk with God.

One thing is sure; if you and I do not seek to both enjoy the delight of this life as well as keep the rules of God while doing so, we will miss our calling. And, one day when you and I are not paying attention, the dogs of this world may just knock us down! Well, I'd better go load Princess up, get Jasper, and go for a walk. I'll look both ways when they're racing around! You keep your eyes open too!

The Day I Killed the Sparrow

My slingshot was my prized possession. I expect most of you men can identify with that statement if you think back to your boyhood days. Whenever I am out in the woods, I still find myself noticing the forks in tree limbs--still searching for the perfect slingshot handle! I grew up in the post-World War II years, when "genuine red rubber" inner tubes were hard to come by—we were getting that sorry synthetic stuff! We boys would search every filling station and tire dealer for a red rubber tube, from which we cut strips to fasten to our cherished slingshot handle. Our favorite pastime was hunting, of course.

I still remember a scene from those long-ago days when I must have been either *very* young or extremely gullible. It was right after lunch; my mother was rocking a younger brother, and I was itching to get my slingshot and start out. My mother persuaded me to take a nap because, as she pointed out very logically, if I would wait a bit longer and let all the birds eat a big lunch, they would fly slower and my luck would be better! But I never really hit anything—either the rocks were not right, the forked handle was no good, or the rubber bands broke. But one day which is still so clear—I shot a bird. I remember seeing it in the shrubbery hedge; sneaking up on it; fitting a rock and pulling back; and the bird fell. I was smitten with feelings of unbelief, then of remorse and guilt. I did not even go up to look at the bird. It may have been just a sparrow.

How important was that one little bird? Turn in your Bible to Matthew 10:28-31. Jesus is talking here about sparrows. The Greek word for sparrow is *strouthion,* which means little bird." It is a diminutive of *strouthos,* which means "bird," and the word may come from the Greek word meaning "to twitter." So a sparrow is a "little twitterer!" Do you know why Jesus is talking about the falling sparrow in this passage? Because He was about to send the disciples out into the world to teach and preach and live out the Gospel—and they would often feel like sparrows! With no influence, no worth, no power, no uniqueness. And they would be preaching to people who also felt like sparrows—no influence, no worth, no power, no special character.

Who do the Gospel writers say heard Jesus gladly? The sparrows!—the poor, the publicans, the sinners, the outcasts. Those with no power, no influence, no worth, no uniqueness. Who does Paul say in 1 Corinthians makes up the church? "not many wise after the flesh, not many mighty, not many noble."—The sparrows, that's who!

Some folks feel like sparrows all the time; all of us feel like sparrows some of the time. Last I heard, one half of all traffic deaths involve drinking drivers--and the 25,000 innocent victims yearly are fathers, mothers, and children . . . sparrows that fall. The young blue-collar worker or middle-rung young white collar executive who gets a pink slip without warning or compassion from a huge company—sparrows that fall. In the raging storm of divorce so common in our nation, one of every two marriages will fail. Sparrows that fall. The soldier who comes back in a box—and many who look all right—sparrows that fall.

Jesus used the illustration of the sparrow because they are *so expendable.* Matthew says two of them sold for one cent; Luke says five would sell for two cents—a bargain, that! Actually the coin mentioned here was the smallest copper coin in that time; it took sixteen of them to make a denairus. Who wanted sparrows? They were cheap. Who valued them? Little boys to shoot at. . . cats to slink about and kill.

What did Jesus say about our sparrow complex? He said *even the sparrow has value to God.* We tend to say, "what is a sparrow compared to the mighty eagle?" Did you ever see a sparrow's image on a coin? Can you imagine the sparrow as the symbol of the U.S. Mail? Can you imagine a golden sparrow adorning our flagpoles? What is a sparrow compared to the graceful swan? Can the sparrow's colors compete with those of the gorgeous cardinal, or even those of the noisy blue jay? In fact, about the only value men see in sparrows is their dubious use as a poor man's food.

But God cares about the sparrow. The Biblical word here for value in Matthew 10:31 and Luke 12:7 has to do with being different, unique! Now Jesus is really not talking about sparrows, but about people--common, plain, ordinary people as we see them. But we are all valuable to God because each of us is different, unique, shaped so by the hand of God. Jesus said *God knows what happens even to the sparrow.* Luke 12:6 beautifully expresses this truth in these words: ". . .not one of them is forgotten before God."

There is one Old Testament reference to the sparrow in the Bible—it is found in Psalm 84: *How lovely are thy tabernacles, O Lord of hosts! My soul longeth, yea, even fainteth for the courts of the Lord: my heart and my flesh crieth out for the living God. Yea, the sparrow hath found a home . . . where she may lay her young, even thine altars, O Lord of Hosts, my King, and my God.*

Let's all us sparrows build our nest in the House of the Lord.

Yellow Jacket Stings

Well, old man Winter is just around the corner. All the wildflowers are gone, the stalks cut down, the mulching done. I saw a great big hornet's nest high in a tree in my yard now that the leaves are almost all fallen. If you didn't get up to the Ridge you missed a spectacular color show. But now it's time to rake or blow the leaves. My neighbor was out raking the other day and stirred up a whole mess of yellow jackets. One of them popped him. I told him it was nothing; why, a real man just brushes that away like a mosquito bite. He didn't buy that. And seriously, many folks are allergic to insect stings and can get in real trouble.

But, back in the days when we didn't know about allergies and such, about 40 or so years ago, I really got clobbered by those little yellow jackets. We were pastoring in Florida and vacationing in north Georgia, at a lovely place called lake Conasauga. You've heard of it? Well, it's at the top of the mountain, perhaps 15 winding miles on a gravel switch-back road from the nearest town, or was back then. The forestry rangers even provided the firewood, the place was so isolated. Well, I was out chopping up some firewood late one afternoon when suddenly the air was filled with yellow jackets, and before I could figure out if they were nesting among the piled firewood or in some hole in the ground, I had been stung by a passel of 'em.

I made my way over to our tent and told my wife I might be dying. Well, we were both still in our twenties and knew little about home remedies and such. We didn't have anything to put on the stings—I remember counting 23 stings, and she remembers only 19, so what's new. Anyhow, my wife went from tent to tent among the other ten camping families. In the meantime I lay down on the cot and pondered life and death. To make a long story short, she came back in a few minutes with a neighbor or two and a collection of home remedies. Some, like putting a paste of chewing tobacco on each sting, I tried. (Others, unmentioned, I did not try.) I lived and had no ill effects beyond some itching the next few days. I now know I was fortunate.

I tell that story to say that what I remember most vividly were my thoughts as I lay on the cot in the tent. I thought, "I'm going to die. Sure as God made little green apples, these stings are going to kill me!" I had never heard of anyone being stung 23 times and walking away from it. I began to get my spiritual house in order. You'd think a minister's spiritual house would be in order, wouldn't you? Anyhow, I began to think about what was most important in life, what I most dreaded to leave behind, what my relationship to God was, and those sort of things. It was a good exercise. One that I have not forgotten forty years later.

But you know, it ought not take that kind of scare to get us to evaluate our lives. They say that a dying person's life flashes before their eyes. Our lives—the integrity of it, the stuff that makes it up, the decisions that shape our ends, the values that keep us on course, the loved ones who share our deepest experiences—these ought to be examined and reaffirmed daily.

Some people do a life-check each Sunday when they kneel in the pew at church. Some folks get to thinking deep thoughts out in a duck blind or a deer stand. Surely year's end, birthdays, family reunions and that sort of thing are occasions for deep thoughts. But you know, maybe right now is a good time. It may be your last time.

A Bit of Snake Theology

It was 1950. I was 12 years old when it happened; I remember it as if it were yesterday. The news was like thunder: Snakebite! Two of my uncles had been chopping wood when a huge rattlesnake bit one of them. The other uncle applied a tourniquet, got him in the truck and raced for the hospital, some 30 miles away. That night he died. The next day a group of us kids went down to the woods behind my grandparents' house where it had happened, to see the snake, and the gate they drove through, and to talk about it all in the way young boys do. It was a huge snake—bigger than two hands would reach around, and over six feet long. Ever since that time I have been in a state of war with snakes.

Most folks have a fear of snakes, yet there is a little story about snakes, found in Numbers 21:6-9, which leads to a much bigger story. Moses has led the children of Israel out of Egypt, and now, nearing the end of the forty years of wandering, the people's song is still the same—simply the fortieth verse: a murmuring, griping, complaining people. Their "soul was short" (21:4), and they loathed that "light bread"—the manna (21:5). Moses was mighty tired of their grumbling, and apparently God got tired of it, too, and sent a punishment upon them. And a terrible punishment it was—fiery serpents which bit the people. Bit them when they least expected; falling to die in fiery fever and agony. The sight that saved the people was a bronze snake, fastened on top of a long pole, and held high as Moses walked through the camp. What a vivid scene—the sick, feverish, convulsed ones lifting their eyes to behold the image of their misery—the bronze serpent! And all who looked, lived!

It is the Advent season, a kindred season of hope and expectation. These are days in which we focus on our need for repentance and deeper commitment, days in which we magnify the hope and expectation we have in Christ.

And this story of the snake is an Advent story, a story leading to a bigger snake story in the New Testament. Three times, in John's Gospel, we note references to this story. The first mention is in chapter 3 in the meeting of Jesus with Nicodemus. Here is a good man, a ruler of the Jews, who understands neither how the wind blows nor how the new birth can be. So, to put it in terms more familiar to him, Jesus gives a new interpretation of the old story of the snakes— "And as Moses lifted up the serpent in the wilderness, even so must the Son of Man be lifted up; that whoever believes in him may have eternal life." The Advent message for us is that head knowledge alone won't cut it. We will never find salvation through our own efforts or intelligence.

The second use of the story by Jesus is seen in John 8, as Jesus talks with the Pharisees: "I said therefore to you, that you shall die in your sins; for unless you believe that I am He, you shall die in your sins...When you lift up the Son of Man, then you will know that I am He..." (vv. 24, 28). In this passage, Jesus uses this story to witness to his enemies, and the truth for them and for us is clear: in the garden we received more than fruit and talk from the serpent; we received the poison of his lies and trusted ourselves rather than our Maker. We are bitten by the serpent, and unless we believe, we will die in our sins. Advent is a time to reflect on the meaning of the snake in the garden, and acknowledge our sick condition.

The third use of the story is found in the twelfth chapter of John, as the Greeks say to Philip, "Sir, we would see Jesus." With their coming Jesus knew His hour had come, and says, "And I, if I be lifted up from the earth, will draw all men to Myself" (12:32). Here is the universal need, and the universal salvation. Advent is about all kinds of folks responding to the call of their hearts to seek the healing manger; Wise Men, shepherds, you and me.

The great British preacher, Charles Spurgeon, used to tell of his conversion. He was 16, living with his grandparents. It was snowing heavily that Sunday morning, but he decided to go to church anyhow. The snow was so deep he turned aside to a little Primitive Methodist Church. There were only 15 people there; even the preacher was snowbound and absent. A layman got up and preached from Isaiah 45:22: "Look unto me, and be ye saved, all the ends of the earth: for I am God, and there is none else." Spurgeon said the man kept saying over and over, "Look, look, look!" and Spurgeon looked, and lived. The 60,000 persons who filed by his coffin at his death in 1892, and the 12,000 people who followed his coffin to the graveyard and watched it lowered into the grave, saw on top of it a Bible, open to this verse of his conversion: "Look unto me, and be ye saved...That's the message of the snake story in the Old Testament as Moses lifted up the serpent; that's the message in the New Testament as Jesus was lifted up.

 Chapter Two

A Pastor's Pilgrimage

Could You Describe a Minister?

I got to musing the other day about how preachers are viewed by the general public. Funny thing that in the movies most professions are depicted halfway truthfully, but two groups are skewed. The prostitute and the preacher. The prostitute is always pictured in the movies as a good-hearted person, who has strength of character and helps the underdog, etc. etc. The preacher? He's usually a harmless, ridiculous, irrelevant, bumbling figure who mumbles inane phrases at the funerals depicted in movies, or else in the movie he gives a stirring 30 second sermon totally devoid of any Biblical content.

How do you picture preachers, "reverends", or whatever you call them? It is true that the office of pastor, preacher, minister has been tarnished by the scandals of some television preachers, but that is only a very small percentage of these men and women. Let me talk with you a moment about the personal life and calling of ministers.

Like myself, most ministers are in this work because they have felt a call from God. The joke about the man seeing the letters "GP" in the sky and interpreting it as God saying, "Go Preach" when it really meant "Go Plow" has some merit to it, but not often. Most ministers enter the ministry without any thought of whether they will ever get rich that way. Most ministers feel a calling, in the words of the mission of the Wilkesboro Baptist Church, "to minister to the weary in need of rest, to the lonely in need of friendship, to the hurting in need of comfort, to the sinful in need of a Savior, and to the joyful in need of a place of celebration."

But in this age of television, even the pastor of the smallest country church is expected to be a fine speaker, a good administrator, a supurb counselor, a genius at public relations for the church, husband to the perfect wife (meaning she is involved in everything at the church), father of perfect children (meaning they will never act like the deacons' children and be arrested for drunk driving, etc. etc.). He is to visit every home once a week, be sure to see all those in the hospital, even if the hospital is a couple hundred miles away, and somewhere along the way he is to prepare honest messages from God given to him as he meditates and studies the Word of God. Can any man—or woman—fit that picture?

I had just gone to a new pastorate of about 2000 members, and after a few months, a terrible tragedy happened. Several teenagers in the church were involved in a car crash. My wife and I had spent the night in Atlanta at the hospital with the families, trying to bring comfort in the deaths of several of the youth. We finally headed back to our town the next morning. We stopped by a grocery to pick up a few items. In line to check out, an elderly church member saw us and demanded if the new pastor knew her name. It was absolutely the wrong thing for her to do! With no sleep, with the horrible night still fresh—I put down the groceries, told the stunned cashier, "If you know her name, you tell her!" and walked out. Naturally, a few minutes later I was aghast at what I had done and called my secretary, who was a walking bank of information. I described the lady to her, she immediately gave me all kinds of personal information on that lady—family, birthdays, anniversaries, etc. So I went to the lady's home to apologize and see if I could mend the fence. When she came to the door, you would have thought she was seeing a ghost! The long and the short of it is that we smoothed it over, and she explained that she had a fear of dying and the pastor not knowing her name!

Remember that your pastor is human. He tries to do his best for you and for God, but like you, he has faults and frailities. Yet such

stories as the above are so easily outweighed by the gratitude of folks whose lives have actually been changed, who have received strength and comfort and hope, as the minister brings the grace of God to situations just by his presence. As the great Baptist minister George Truett said, "If I had a thousand lives, I would spend them as a Baptist preacher."

Ah, it's a great life if you keep your eye on heaven!

The Hinge Time

This little girl is very talkative, and indeed, bright beyond her years. In fact, I first met her when I talked with the committee seeking an interim pastor for their church. Her father was a part of that committee, and after they and I had talked for while and the committee needed to huddle to make a decision, she was assigned to get my wife and me a coke and show us the sanctuary.

We got the full tour of the church, including the "special" room, the baptistry. I think most children look forward with a delicious fear to the day when they will be baptized. And we saw the pastor's study, the room, said she to me, "where you'll stay." Just like I was a book or a pot or a pan to be put somewhere until needed.

Well, I've been the interim pastor at that church for over six months now, and yesterday she came up to me and said, "Are you going to be here forever?" I didn't pursue whether or not she thought that would be a good idea! I did assure her that a committee was seeking a permanent pastor and that I would not be staying forever. She came back later to tell me she thought it would be nice if I stayed forever.

Which incident leads me to muse on this business of being an interim pastor. Who knows, perhaps some folks in dealing with an interim period in their church will find a thought or two to ponder. My first thought is that interim periods are not all bad. Even churches need a change in leadership from time to time. So if you're in an interim time at your church, keep the good memories of the past leadership and move on with a fresh vision toward the coming of a new pastor.

I feel the interim time, the hinge time, the time between full-time pastors at a church, is a time for reflection, appreciation of the past, and a time to appreciate change. Some churches shy away from change during an interim; I think that's too bad. In the interim time the past can be evaluated, a vision for the future can be forged, a direction can be shaped, and some of the low-hanging fruit of the new vision can even be gathered. The interim time does not have to be a sad or low period.

As an interim pastor, I try to lead the congregation to understand that the new pastor will not be the same person as the previous pastor. In fact, I like to make a few changes—with as little repercussion as possible—to help the people realize that the future will not be just like the past, no matter how good that was.

Sometimes there are staff situations that need to be dealt with. Some churches tread water on these and other situations that might be divisive, waiting to dump these problems on the new pastor. That seems quite unfair. Why should the new pastor have a strike against him at the start?

For me, serving as an interim pastor—I'm in my seventh since "retiring" six years ago—is a delight and joy. I've made many new friends in the Boone, Lenoir, and West Jefferson area. As an interim pastor, I have all the joys and few of the headaches of the pastorate. I get to preach sermons from the past that have proved helpful to folks; I get to serve as a consultant for the church as they seek a pastor; and I generally get to leave before I get into trouble!

You can't beat that with a stick! So go enjoy the interim pastor!

When's the Last Time . . .

A week or so ago I celebrated my 39th birthday for the 28th time. The folks at the fine church where I serve as interim pastor found out about it, and surprised the wife and me with a covered-dish luncheon after morning worship. But that wasn't all—they "pounded" us with all kinds of canned goods, paper goods, jellies (home canned), candies, and even flowers to plant in my garden! I haven't been pounded in about 40 years—not since my seminary church. Did I ever tell you about that church?

One saint in that little church of 99 members was Mrs. Elva Coleman. If she has any extended relatives in this newspaper's coverage area, I want you to know how much she meant to us back then, and that her memory is still sacred. I went to the little church just over the line in Virginia as a green, 22-year-old preacher boy in his first year of seminary. The little parsonage needed some repairs, so Pegeen and I stayed with Mrs. Coleman for several weekends. I will never forget the first weekend; it still stands out as one of life's most embarrassing moments! It was Sunday afternoon, and Pegeen and I were relaxing in our bedroom. I say relaxing, but it was a bit difficult to do in a room filled with antique furniture. We were lying on the bed, Pegeen was studying her "Training Union" lesson (for those of you who are old Baptists) and I was going over the Sunday evening sermon. Suddenly the beautiful antique bed on which we were lying collapsed! Here we were, the new minister and his wife, married less than a year, staying in the home of a genuine Virginia gentry widow, and the bed falls down! I couldn't imagine what she would think when I tried to explain!

I went over to her side of the house, knocked on the door until I roused the poor soul who was trying to catch an afternoon nap. I explained that we were minding our own business, studying the Bible and all that, when the bed fell down. I apologized profusely, offered to pay for any damages—and the beautiful antique wash basin and pitcher under the bed certainly had damages—and asked for a hammer with which I could put the bed back together. I will never forget her reaction. Was either of us hurt? No? Well, thank God. And as for borrowing the hammer—that was unthinkable on the Sabbath! No problem, since we were going back to seminary after the evening service. Forget the wash basin and pitcher, relax in the parlor and have a good afternoon!

Mrs. Coleman used to fix Sunday lunch for us often in the days that followed. She had a large screened veranda, and Sunday lunch—she called it dinner—was a real production. She always prepared several vegetables, at least three meats, homemade rolls, iced tea with sprigs of mint in it, and a couple of desserts. Man, that woman could make a caramel pie! And all of this for three people. When our first child was born, Mrs. Coleman gave us an antique baby carriage. In later years when we visited her, she always insisted we go behind the house down the slope to the spring. There we would always clean the spring out, and drink the cool, pure water. Best in the valley.

Mrs. Coleman is gone now, but her kindnesses to a young, inexperienced pastor and his wife will remain a warm memory as long as my wife and I live. She was one of those folks who knew life is too short to criticize the pastor, that most pastors are doing the best they can, and that encouragement would help him grow and mature in the high office of minister.

How long has it been since you said a word of encouragement to your pastor? Or invited him and his wife out to dinner—for no reason at all except to say, "We appreciate you." If you want to be remembered with warmth and gratitude for decades, that's the way to do it. God bless all Mrs. Colemans.

Have You Counted the Cost Lately?

I was thinking of Brother Arvin Stith the other day. It's been 40 years since Brother Arvin came into my life. I don't guess he'll ever leave as long as I live. He was—and is—one of those characters who seem almost too large for life. While I was in seminary in Kentucky, I was called as pastor of a church in a small town. When I say small, I mean small—the name of the town (A Philistine city in the Bible) was written on both sides of the sign welcoming you to the village.

The church building was about as old as most of the congregation, and that was old. Two old potbellied stoves warmed the sanctuary. One of them had a large split at about its belt-line. You could look in and see the coal burning. So, to keep coals from falling out the split during the sermon, one of the deacons would come forward to the stove during the choir special, select some extra large pieces of coal, and stoke up the fire with them so they would last through the sermon. It usually worked.

The day finally came when the little church decided to build a new building. They had been working on a building fund for something like 30 years. Well, we got plans drawn up, committees met until they were blue in the face. Meanwhile, I was carpooling every day to Louisville to seminary, some fifty miles away. Every afternoon as I came back into the village I would stop by the post office, which was in a family's home.

And, most every day, there would be a note from Brother Arvin. Sometimes it would be a pithy statement of how a man of God ought to have better sense than to do what I was doing in agreeing to build a new church building. Sometimes Brother Arvin buttressed his argument with scriptures like the one about starting out to build a tower and running out of money. That one always got my attention. He also used the one about going to war against an army twice the size as yours, and similar such scriptures.

Well, finally the day came to vote on whether to build the new building. The place was crowded—you would have thought it was somebody's funeral, the place was that crowded. We took up the offering early, so as to have the plates ready for the folks to place their ballot in them later in the service. After the vote, we asked one of the half-dozen or so deacons to come forward, pull a chair up to the communion table, and count the votes.

It was the kind of scene you never forget. Brother Harold—the deacon asked to count the votes in front of everybody—was single, having never married. He was overly conscientious anyway, and this task really put pressure on him. Ballot by ballot, he opened the slips of paper and read aloud the verdict, with the sweat pouring down his face. He wasn't the only one sweating. The vote was 92 for building, and 4 for not building. It really didn't take a genius to figure out who the "No" votes were, and in good Baptist fashion we forged ahead with our project. Today there is a beautiful sanctuary, and few people remember the tension of that day long ago.

As the workmen tore the old building down, our son who was only two or three years old, was very upset that they were tearing the church down. On one of the massive floor joists I saw written, "Arvin Stith", in large letters. Brother Arvin had been one of the carpenters on the church back in 1904.

Brother Arvin broke his hip a few months later. Smashed it like an eggshell, the city doctor said. They put in a stainless-steel ball and socket, or so they said. Brother Arvin was fit to be tied. He lived next door to the church, and he was accustomed to being there when the doors opened. He missed three Sundays at church on account of that hip, and came back growling that he couldn't get up the steps into the choir loft. He sang bass.

Well, after four years I graduated from seminary and left for an-

other pastorate. Brother Arvin left not too long afterwards, heading for heaven. But I still think about his words every now and then. I don't apply them to building a new church building—I apply them to the decision to follow Christ. I think about how many folks through the years I've seen start out on the Christian pilgrimage and not have the commitment to stay with it; not have the love for Christ and his church that it takes to make a good witness before the world. It's a shame. I liked the honest opposition of Brother Arvin better.

Take a moment and count the cost. How are you doing?

Fires and Gratitude

I know it will make you jealous, but I'm going to tell you anyhow! I've been having a fire in the fireplace in the evenings for a week or two now, since the nights have gotten nippy. By the way, we had a sprinkling of snow last Sunday. I do declare that there are few pleasures in life that rank with building a good fire and enjoying it as you watch the snow, read a good book and listen to great music, or even watch a football game or movie. But you must build the fire right in order to feel justly superior about it.

No fair using newspaper to start a fire. Can you imagine people doing that? And obviously a gas flame to help the fire along is cheating in a way that I know you wouldn't do. Now, first, you get some "fat lightard". You probably know whereof I speak; this is pine wood that is full of pitch, and burns like crazy. A splinter of it is enough to start your fire, if you place your kindling wood right. On top of the kindling you can put your smaller pieces of oak or locust, or whatever, and then the larger pieces of firewood. Now make sure the damper is open, light the fat lightard, and settle back for a fine evening.

Speaking of fires and winter evenings, it was a cold, snowy evening in western Kentucky. I was a young graduate student with more commitment to my church than good sense, and so I was out making the obligatory two pastoral visits per evening. By day I car-pooled to Louisville to attend the seminary, and after I returned each afternoon and had supper, I visited church members. This particular visit was to an elderly couple whose home was of the "humble abode" variety.

As I entered the home, there were the usual food smells and other odors dominant in a home tightly shut and overly warm against the winter wind. A fire was blazing in the fireplace, and seeing the gentleman of the house with his chair pulled up to the fire, and his wife pulling hers up to the fireplace even as she bade me do likewise, I too pulled a wooden rocker close to the fire and stared at the coals for awhile.

The old gentleman was a man of few words, possibly due to the wad of tobacco he spit regularly into the fire, and my conversation was mostly with the wife. However, as we tried to pass the pleasantries, the husband began to get a "coughing fit", as we used to call it. Both the wife and I ignored the situation as long as we could, but the noise made conversation well nigh impossible.

Finally the good wife said to me, "I keep telling Jim to stop that coughing! In fact, if he keeps it up, I told him we will have to go to the hospital, and they'll take out his lung." Turning to me, she said in a whisper, "They've already taken out one lung, you know." Well, I kept a straight face although I couldn't help thinking, "he doesn't know what trouble is until they take out that one remaining lung!"

For the first few years, that incident struck me as both sad and funny, because the wife didn't seem to realize what she was saying. But as the years went by, I reflected on how much all of us who enjoy good health are blessed. Henry Ford used to say, when due to health he had to eat only bread and milk, that he would give a fortune to have a good meal! Money cannot buy the most meaningful things in life. I'm grateful to health, for friends, for each day in which to praise God and seek to do my bit part in His kingdom.

For what are you grateful this Thanksgiving? Build a good fire and ponder it.

Blooming Where You Are

Summer is upon us, and 'tis the season for moving again. Somewhere I read that one-third of American families move every three years or so. I do believe it. And, along with the raise in pay and more responsibilities and the new house also comes the adjustment to a new community, new schools, new churches, new friends—and saying goodbye to the old ones. Depression is often a part of the change. How does one cope with this kind of necessary change when our emotions are in turmoil?

Let me tell you a story. A long time ago, just after we were married, Pegeen and I visited her elderly grandmother in Florida. As we were leaving after a delightful visit she led us to her bedroom to show us an unusual sight. There, growing out of the wall receptacle, was a green vine perhaps three feet long, stretching forth toward the light! She said, "I have been living here for over 12 years, and I know there has been no daylight down underneath the floor for at least that long. Yet in the last year or so I have had to keep snipping that plant off time and again, or it would bloom!"

What a parable of life that is! How necessary and how hard to bloom where you are! In the Book of Acts we find the story of two remarkable saints, Priscilla and Aquila. Here is a couple raised in one place, Asia Minor, as home. But we find them living in Rome, then in Corinth, then in Ephesus, and then back to Rome, and back again to Ephesus. And all these moves happened in the space of 8 or 10 years—they moved every year or two! Yet they always bloomed where they were.

Blooming wherever we are is a matter of the will and faith. And I do not speak only of the problems of blooming where you are when you move from one place to another; there is the challenge of blooming in a new situation and a new environment when an illness or the reality of growing old or personal tragedy or family crisis demands changes in our lives. *It can be done; like the vine struggling toward the light, we can bloom where we are.* I look into the Bible and see Abraham, who went out at God's bidding, leaving family and friends. His story is one of a man who bloomed wherever he was. And there is Joseph, who is a vine struggling to bloom wherever he found himself. And then we see Moses, blooming wherever he is, in the courts of Pharaoh and on the hills of Arabia and in the desert of Sinai. And time fails us to speak of Daniel, who bloomed in the exile.

I think of John Bunyan, the author of that Christian classic, *Pilgrim's Progress,* which had a place next to the Bible in homes of faith for three centuries. Bunyan was cast into prison for preaching the gospel, and in that dark dungeon he bloomed, spending the 12 years writing *Pilgrim's Progress.* You can bloom wherever you are. There is another classic on my shelves, a slim volume entitled *The Practice of the Presence of God,* written by Brother Lawrence, a monk who was no good at preaching, but he could serve God and bloom in the kitchen of the monastery, preparing the meals for the other men. You can bloom if you choose to put down roots wherever you are.

There are three requirements to blooming where you are, and they have to do with our will and our faith. To bloom wherever we are, we must *(1) put down roots; (2) reach up to the light of God's presence; and (3) we must have a desire to be helpful.*

Sometimes when Christian families move to a new community they hang back and "church shop" until the devil gets them out of the habit of going to church. I think the devil would rather neutralize a hard-working, church-oriented Christian couple than to win over the soul of a hardened sinner anyway. Don't make that mistake if you are new in the community. Pray, visit the churches you feel may be right for you, and then make a decision and a commitment to get involved in

a church.

And, if you're about to move to some other community, remember that you can bloom there. The Syrian General Naaman in the Old Testament was converted to the worship of Israel's God when he was healed of leprosy. He then desired to carry a donkey load of earth from Palestine to Syria, so Israel's God could be powerful there, too. You know better than that—the Lord God is everywhere. You can serve Him wherever you go.

Okay, little green vine—head for the light!

A Word on Behalf of Ministers

Things are tough all over, but since October is Pastor Appreciation Month, let me muse on the situation of one group in our society—ministers. Just to show you how simple-minded I am, it was not until the era of the Jim Bakker scandal and the fall of other television evangelists that I ever considered that a minister would be in this work for money! I'm serious. *(You say you could have enlightened me?)* When I felt a call of God to go into the ministry in 1955, as a 17 year-old-boy, I poured my soul and my life and all my ambition into being the best possible minister I could be. I felt a call to preach was a call to prepare. I went to college thinking I was dumb and the professors would help me get a handle on how to understand and preach the Good News of Jesus. I shall always be grateful to committed, open-minded teachers of religion for their blessing on my life. After 11 years of college and seminary and a Ph.D. degree in theology and 15 years in churches, I had not moved a smidgeon from my view that nobody would go into the ministry for money.

As any pastor will tell you, a few years in the pastorate will convince you that the ministry is not the place to get rich! But then, I didn't expect to get rich. Like so many other ministers, I paid into an annuity fund and expected God and the annuity board to take care of me in old age. God has certainly done his part . . .I am blessed to have a lovely retirement home in Blowing Rock, to have the privilege of preaching every Sunday either as interim or some special teaching occasion, and to have many friends.

Now consider your pastor. If he's a true man of God, he'll not be money-oriented. He'll probably not say anything when the church adds up *everything* it costs the church to have a minister and gives the impression that the total amount is his salary. He will no doubt keep silent even though out of that "outrageous salary we're pay-ing the preacher" he must take his social security, his hospitaliza-tion insurance, his life insurance, his retirement, his travel expenses, any continuing education—in short, things that in the business world are considered "benefits" over and above the salary. And a laughable thing about it all is that the minister is considered by the government to be "self-employed" which means he pays a higher bracket of social security! *But hear me saying that he won't mention that kind of thing to you.* But I can.

I think I'm a fairly typical minister. I've been glad to serve the church day and night for 40 plus years. The part of my work that most people see—the sermons—has been done at night after 8-10 hour days for these 40 years. After a while I tried to make it a point to take a day off each week. My family has been neglected, I suppose. But both my children are strong Christians and active in churches, and my wife feels as much called to the ministry as I. So I have no sour grapes at all. It's been a wonderful experience, and I wouldn't want to be anyting but a pastor. But can I suggest some things you can do for *your* pastor to show that you appreciate his commitment to God and to your church?

Being stingy as a church won't make him a better pastor. *"Lord, you keep him humble and we'll keep him poor"* is not an appropri-ate prayer! So expect your pastor to work hard, and pay him well. It won't turn his head; in fact I believe that the way to get rid of a pastor

you don't like is to shower him with kindness—he'll work himself to death! Pastors also appreciate the kind deed—an invitation to dinner, the birthday remembrance, etc.—or just a compliment for no reason at all except that you love and appreciate God's servant. And, don't forget to pray for your pastor. Ask God to give him good health, a love for his flock, safety for his family . . .

And one other thing. The pastor's wife can be the loneliest woman in town. Ladies, befriend her. She already lives in a glass house, so overlook shortcomings. Look for things to compliment, not to criticize. And the church will be blessed.   Selah.

The Story of a Sermon

One of those things that really bugs me is to go to a church, pick up a bulletin to see what the pastor is preaching on this morning, and find a big blank space where the sermon title ought to be. Now I know I shouldn't be critical, because there are many reasons why a pastor might not list his sermon title. Perhaps he doesn't give a title to his sermons—my wife doesn't title her sermons to me! Perhaps he feels the congregation wouldn't appreciate knowing the title—maybe he figures they can't read, or perhaps he feels they might walk out if they see the topic ahead of time! I've heard of pastors who say they give no sermon title because if they did, the devil could get hold of the sermon and twist it. You know, there's something in all those reasons . . . yet the devil in me says the pastor simply doesn't have a sermon title ready in time for the printing of the bulletin!

But on to better things. Have you ever wondered how your pastor prepares his sermons? I'll share with you how I have gone about that labor and joy for over 40 years. But first, let me say I marvel at the fact that for all those years I started over every Monday morning putting a sermon together, and always, always felt a thrill in that task.

Here's how I do it. First, I have a notebook filled with sermon ideas. Anything I read, hear someone say, stumble over on the internet, become aware of in my devotional reading and prayers that strikes a chord for a sermon, I write in that notebook. I go back through that notebook regularly, and I pluck the sermon idea that's ripe. In my pastorates I have enjoyed doing sermon series—on Biblical characters, on prayer, on the Sermon on the Mount, preaching through a book of the Bible, that sort of thing. But a lot of my preaching is topical; that is, I may start from an incident in our time and take it back to a Biblical principle. For instance, while traveling in Switzerland some years ago, I was struck by the inscriptions in the cemetery at Zermatt, the jumping-off place for those who try to climb the Matterhorn. The folks buried there who died on the mountain came from all over the world—"born in India, died on the Matterhorn"; three friends from Oxford University in England, a 17-year-old from New York—and on and on. It struck me that the pearl merchant in Jesus' parable about the pearl of great price was pulled to seek the pearl just like that! And so was born the sermon "The Pull of the Pearl."

I take my idea, brainstorm it from Monday until about Wednesday, clarifying what I want to say, letting scripture, stories and illustrations float up to the surface of my mind. Then I turn to my Biblical commentaries and see what scholars and preachers through the years have had to say on this scripture. I never go to the commentaries first. I always had the sermon title and text ready by Thursday for the secretary to put in the Sunday bulletin. On Friday—or, God forbid, on Saturday—I would sit down at the typewriter, or in recent years at the computer, and write out my sermon, word for word. This allowed me to choose my words carefully and to see what I was saying in print.

One important practice I have had through the years as I write the sermon—and I write it in a spoken style so it reads as a conversation—is to imagine a church member saying what I am saying. I imagine a church member who I trust, one who is a mature Christian,

saying what this sermon is saying. And I ask myself, "Is this scriptural? Is this helpful to this church at this time? Is this as clear as I can say this? Is this as forceful as I need to say this?" I have always used two words when possible rather than one long one! I figure if the kids can understand the sermon, then perhaps most of the adults can as well.

I then deliver the sermon without any notes, having gotten up early on Sunday morning for prayer, meditation and study of the manuscript. This lets me have a freedom to look the people in the eye. It helps to be able to see the manuscript, as I usually can, in my mind's eye. And then, the sermon is available in printed form the following Sunday.

Well, that's my approach to sermons. Usually the folks stay awake. And, by the way, don't use this article as a litmus test of your pastor's preaching. He's probably a better preacher anyway.

How's Your Hearing?

My wife says I'm getting deaf, or as the old folks say, "hard of hearing." Of course she's been saying that ever since we married—that I have selective deafness. She says I can hear other people, but cannot hear her when there's a "honey-do" project ahead! That's really not true . . . not all of the time. This business of hearing got me to thinking.

On the Romantic Road of Germany, where I am as you read this article, there are several quaint old walled cities left over from medieval times. Rothenburg at the top of the Road, then Nordlingen, then Dinklesbuhl on down toward Munich and the delightful little rococo church in the field at Wies. One time my wife and I were spending the evening in the village of Nordlingen. We were staying in an old hotel, a favorite long ago of touring kings and queens, with its creaking, slanting stairways. We had read about the church in the very center of town, from which all the streets spread out like spokes of a wheel. The church has a tall tower, locally known as "the Daniel." A night watchman lives at the top of the 350 steps up to the top of the "Daniel." A special tourist attraction is to stand down in the street and see the watchman open the window at the top of the tower at the strike of the hour and proclaim that all is well.

So, we hurried through our supper and I joined the crowd gathering outside our hotel, just across the street from the church. Slowly the tower clock's hands moved to the hour. There was a silence, then the clock marked the hour in deep tones. The shutters of the watchman's window were flung open, the light pouring out behind the figure leaning out the window. He put his hands to his mouth to shout to us who waited expectantly—and as he spoke, several motorcycles roared by!

I couldn't hear a single word the watchman said! Well, in this case I felt I knew what the message was. But I have pondered that incident many times. Is it a parable of the relationship that so many of us have with God? We say we belong to God, and we really mean it. And we say we want to hear what God wants to say to us—through prayer, through the study of His Word, through the church relationship we cherish.

But there's a problem. Far too often, we cannot hear what God is saying to us because of the "background noise." Because of the motorcycles, so to speak. We cannot hear God because our prejudices or our traditions or our past get in our way and make us deaf to hear some life-changing word from God. We find we are distracted from hearing God in worship on a regular basis because the world is beckoning to us, screaming to us, roaring and drowning out the voice of God.

What is the world saying? Simply that while your faith is fine, you need to be out enjoying the beauty of nature; you need to be at

the races or the football game, or at any one of a dozen places on the Lord's Day instead of in church. After all, reasons the world, you work hard, you deserve to "enjoy" your weekend, and after all, church is a bit dull. How would the world know? It hasn't tried church! And so we often fail to hear what God wants to say to us. Jesus warned more than once about the danger of having ears but not using them. "Him who has ears to hear, let him hear."

Getting Ourselves Ready

I had just been called as pastor of a new church. It was a large, exciting church, in the midst of the growing carpet industry, full of young executives and an exploding population. The pastor before me had only stayed four months—he had really wanted to be a college president, but that seemed to have fallen through, so he accepted the pastorate. Then, as soon as he moved out of the state, the college's board of Trustees promptly elected him as president of the college. So, he was pastor for only four months. The pastor before him had stayed 18 years.

That background fostered a lot of appreciation for me as their next young pastor. In fact, looking back, I could have stayed at that church for my entire ministry and had a wonderful experience—and perhaps I should have! Anyhow, my wife and I had moved to the city, the church was anxious for us to feel at home, and after a couple of Sundays came the Sunday afternoon of the welcoming reception. Folks came through the greeting line gushing about our two young children, complimentary of my wife, saying very supportive things to me. It was heady stuff; a match made in heaven.

Then down the line came a man I later learned to love and appreciate for his sense of humor. But on this day he was a stranger to me. As he shook my hand, he said, "Well, we'll see how smart you are." I had no idea what he was driving at, so I smiled and fell right into the trap. "What do you mean?" I asked. "It's like this," he said, "The second pastor back stayed 18 years and then moved on to be a college president. He wasn't too bright; it took us 18 years to get him ready to be a college president. The fellow just before you stayed only four months before leaving to be a college president. He was a quick learner. We'll see how smart you are, by how long it takes to move you on to a college presidency!"

Well, I stayed six years and did not become a college president. But I have chuckled about his assessment many times. And, you know, as God works in the events of our lives, he is preparing us for something much greater than this life. I don't mean that a long life means you are hard for God to mold; but I do think that the Bible teaches that as we move through life we are to become more and more like Jesus. We are being prepared for a glorious destiny.

In the little letter of I John, we read: "Beloved, we are God's children now; it does not yet appear what we shall be, but we know that when he appears we shall be like him, for we shall see him as he is." I suppose some folks would think a college presidency is a big thing . . . but every Christian is being prepared for something much greater, to be like Christ. Check yourself today. Are you more like Christ now than you were a year ago? Are your actions more Christlike? Are your thoughts more Christlike? Or is God having a difficult time shaping and molding you?

Did He Really Say That?

A few years ago, when our daughter was married with children of her own, in one of those lazy family moments, she told us an amazing story. It's the kind of thing that leaves you laughing and declaring

that your other child, now married and with kids of his own, needs a good spanking! I've forgotten the occasion for the conversation, but our daughter was telling us how she was terrorized by her older brother while growing up. As proof, she told us about the hospital incidents.

While pastoring in Dalton, Georgia, my wife and I would often visit church members in Atlanta hospitals or in nearby Chattanooga hospitals. This was back in the days when you could leave your children in the car while you visited the patients without fear of kidnapping, molestation, etc., etc. Well, our daughter must have been about four or five years old at the time. Here's the deep secret her older brother, probably nine at the time, impressed on her.

Said he in conspiratorial whispers, "We have a brother who's not quite right in the head, and so that's why Mom and Dad come to the hospital so often, to visit with him." But, said he, "You mustn't say anything to Mom about it, or it will make her cry." And sure enough, said our daughter, Mom did look sad when we returned to the car. So, the years passed, we often went to the hospital, and the kids grew up. We had no idea that our little girl was in charge of such a haunting secret! She must have been thirty-five or so when we first heard this tale, and all of us burst out laughing at the idea. "Did he really say that?" "Well," she said, "it was very real to me for years, and quite disturbing. And my brother never did set me straight on that."

That's not all he did, according to our daughter. Back in those days, the clocks in cars made a ticking sound that could be heard even in the back seat. Our son would pester his sister by insisting that the ticking was a bomb, and that if she talked or made any loud noise the bomb would explode, killing both of them! That's one way to have peace and quiet!

It's amazing what goes on behind parents' backs! One way to look at these little incidents decades ago is to say that our son had a great imagination, a fact borne out in his career. But I got to thinking the other day about these incidents from their childhood, and before I stopped smiling it had already struck me that this kind of thing happens all the time in the spiritual realm.

Remember how the disaster in the Garden began? It started with Satan telling convenient lies to Eve. When she relates how God has commanded Adam and her to stay clear of a certain tree in the Garden, we hear Satan saying, "Did God really say that? Well, he just wants to keep you under his thumb . . ." The truth is, Satan continually tells us things that are not true about us, about our brothers and sisters, about God himself. He tells us that we know more than God; he tells us that we're not to blame for sin; he tells us there really is no such thing as sin, or a moral law; he tells us that folks who are not a certain color, or not of our kind, are less valuable to God; he tells us to eat, drink, and be merry, for there is no God and no tomorrow.

But one of my favorite Bible verses, Hebrews 2:14-15, puts the lies of Satan into perspective: "Since the children have flesh and blood, he [Jesus] too shared in their humanity so that by his death he might destroy him who holds the power of death—that is, the devil— and free those who all their lives were held in slavery by their fear of death."

Whether it's children scaring other children with "secrets", or Satan scaring us with the power of death, it feels so good to get out from under that burden! And through the new life that Jesus offers us, we are set free from the fear of death which all our life has loomed over us. Celebrate Easter every day!

Down Memory Lane

Pegeen and I have just returned from a trip down memory lane. The plan was to link up with another couple, friends of nearly 50 years, and go back to Florida to visit our roots and share childhood

experiences. We had all gone to Stetson University in DeLand, Florida, and so our pilgrimage started there. It was bittersweet to see the changes in the school. In fact, my old dorm is no longer there. We visited old stomping grounds at Sarasota, Zephyrhills (yeah, the pure water place) and Madison. Our families have all been in Florida at least 80 years, and my folks fought the Indians under the Spanish before Florida became a US territory.

We visited the usual places—where the old home used to be, and the old church, and where the family is buried, etc. All in all, it was a delightful thing, to show old friends where you grew up. But I suppose the most surprising event of the trip was our search to find Cassia Baptist Church.

Back in 1959-60 when I was a senior at Stetson, a dear friend and professor pulled me aside for a conversation. It was not his first; he was already instrumental in getting my wife and me together! He told me of a small church about 15 miles out of town, Cassia Baptist Church, that needed a pastor. He knew that my preaching experience was largely limited to being the summer college revival preacher the year before. He allowed that I would only be at this church for about 8 months, not long enough for me to mess up the church, or for them to ruin me!

So I was ordained and accepted my first pastorate. The salary was $15 per week, and since that was going to be hard to find, I suggested they just pay me $13.50 and keep the $1.50 tithe! The husband in the other couple who traveled with us on this trek down memory was a fellow "preacher-boy" at Stetson, and helped me at the church in that senior year. He led a revival meeting, in preparation for which we rented the big horns you could put on the top of your car and blast the "good news" of the meeting all over the sand hills of central Florida!

It was at this church that I managed to get through my first baptism. On that day I had lunch with a church family, and was sitting on the front porch reflecting on things when a mean looking dog rounded the corner of the house. I asked the little red-headed daughter of my hosts the name of her dog. Glaring at me seriously she replied, "Bear Dog!" I certainly agreed with the appropriateness of his name. Having broken the ice for conversation, I asked the child if she knew where we would be having the baptism. Back in those days, many country churches didn't have indoor baptistries—or toilets, either. Her response troubled me—"Lake Deep!"

Sure enough, three or four steps brought the water to my chest. But, after almost baptizing the lady with her glasses on, I got through the ceremony. I have photos to prove it!

This church had 13 people attending when I went there as pastor, and about eight months later we had grown to about 50 in attendance. It was an interesting church, both people and building. They used the platoon system of attendance; that is, half of the members came to church on one Sunday, and half the next Sunday. That's because they weren't speaking to each other! Years before, one group put a lock on the door, which the other group promptly shot off. There was a huge grand piano in the little wooden church. It was the biggest piano I have ever seen. The rumour was that Fannie Crosby had played that piano, and that it also had been in various movies. I rather doubt both stories. First, Fannie Crosby was blind, and may not have played any piano, and secondly, there was no way that I could imagine for getting that piano out of the church building. I wondered if they built the church around the piano. During my pastorate there, my traveling friend and I put a cross on the church's steeple, at the cost of yellow-jacket attacks.

On a whim, we decided to drive out to Cassia, and see if the church was still in existence. In Florida, everything changes if you take a nap, so we doubted we could find the church. We doubted it was still in existence. We doubted the building was still standing if there were a church. The area had changed, the road was different, but finally we came to the sign: CASSIA. True, the community name was written on both sides of the sign, but this was it! And there was

the old sand road leading into the woods. And about a hundred yards into the woods was the old church. Just like I left it 49 years ago! The cross was still on the steeple. I peered through the old glass front doors and saw the attendance chart on the wall behind the pulpit (Remember when Baptist churches had those attendance boards?) The attendance for last Sunday was 13, and the Sunday before was 15! Apparently they had not made much progress in these past 50 years.

I would rather have seen a thriving church, reaching the changed community. Because as much as I love some of the things of the past, as Christians we are to face the future. After all, it's going to be much better than the past. So, if you're holding onto the past . . . turn loose. If you don't, you might meet it 50 years down the road.

Chapter Three

Thoughts on Special Days

A Christmas Dilemma

It's a recurring problem, but as the years pile up, it gets bigger. The question: *whether to put up an artificial Christmas tree or a real tree.* [Translate "artificial" as "permanent," "realistic," "pre-lit," or "perfect."] I suppose it's true that the genuine, from-the-woods tree isn't perfect; too many gaps in the branches, either too tall or too short, sticks out on one side, etc. etc. But it is real, and it smells like Christmas when I put it up.

When our kids were small, it was a yearly ritual to take them out into the woods and find the "perfect" tree and cut it, after the considered judgment of both children and with the permission of the land owner. But, time goes by and the kids grow up. A handful of years after the kids left home, I got the bright idea that an artificial tree would be a lot less trouble. But, you know, I no more than got that thing up and decorated until I began to have misgivings! Every time I passed by it, I couldn't help but remember that those limbs weren't real; they were wires covered with only heaven-knows-what.

So, our foray into the world of "permanent, realistic, pre-lit, perfect, artificial" trees lasted only one year. We went back to searching out the perfect live tree. And now, we've come to another Christmas and it's time to get the tree. I was in Walmart the other day, and a perfectly beautiful tree, immaculately decorated with golden balls, greeted me in the lobby. For an instant, the traitor in me came out, and I wondered how much that tree would cost. I resisted the temptation, went out to a tree farm and tied a ribbon on a truly perfect tree. I have made peace now with Christmas.

I suppose I should confess that part of my reasoning this Christmas is that if I really should buy an artificial Christmas tree, the folks in the First Baptist Church, West Jefferson, would probably ride me out of town on a rail and tarred and feathered! After all, Ashe County is the heart of the Christmas tree country and provided the national Christmas tree this year. With even the brief treasonous thoughts about the Walmart tree, it's probably a good thing that I'm finishing up my interim at this church in January—my seventh interim in the area of Boone, Lenoir and West Jefferson.

As I've said before, I have this habit of sermonizing. As I sat musing in my den before an absolutely perfect fire the other night, I thought about this business of choosing either the artificial (and let's face it, the fake) or the genuine thing. And the first thing I knew, I was wondering if God had been faced with that dilemma when he came to this business of Christmas himself. Did he consider not coming as a genuine man; just pretending to be like us and share our troubles?

After all, there have been several heresies over the centuries built on the premise that God really didn't become a human being on that first Christmas. That God really didn't suffer on the cross; that God really didn't choose to die for our sins. That it was all a charade; a fake humanity. (See where musing about artificial or genuine Christmas trees leads you?)

Ah, but the essence of the Christian faith is that God did indeed wrap himself in human flesh, be born the son of a poor peasant girl in the backwater of the Roman empire, suffer all the temptations and trials that we suffer, and be put to a painful death that would try not only the full humanity of the God-man, the Son of God, Jesus, but also wring from fevered lips the cry of desolation on the cross.

I think I'll stick with the genuine Christmas tree this Christmas and every Christmas. And I'll let it remind me that God chose the genuine Christmas gift—the gift of himself as one of us, yet conquering evil.

Excuse me; I have to go decorate a Christmas tree.

That Missing King

As a kid in the church Christmas play, once I got the "orient are" part of the song straight, I much preferred to be a king with a cardboard crown than a lowly shepherd in a bathrobe, or an angel wearing a pinned up sheet with coat hanger wings. Matthew 2 gives us a brief but strong portrait of the these three wise men or kings. The Greek text calls them Magi, the word from which we get magic. It seems they were from Arabia or Persia and were the astrologers, the astronomers, the philosophers, the scientists, the counselors to the kings, and perhaps even kings themselves. The Biblical facts are that these magi saw the unusual star, studied its meaning, set off on a journey following the star, came to Jerusalem and conferred with King Herod, went on to Bethlehem guided by the star, presented their gifts and worshipped the Christ child, and then went back to their land another way.

Now, remembering that only Matthew of the four Gospels mentions these kings, and realizing that each Gospel writer, inspired by the Holy Spirit, selected certain facts surrounding the birth of Jesus to emphasize and highlight: *What, then, is the significance, the message, of the three kings from the east?* They certainly do not seem essential to the story of Jesus' birth. No angel goes to them as they do to Mary and Joseph and the shepherds on the hills; these kings seem to turn up on their own. But notice this: *they symbolize the full significance of the birth of Jesus.* Their gifts characterize the entire life and ministry of Jesus. It is likely that the Holy Spirit intends for us to learn from the kings of the east *three major truths: the royalty of Jesus, the universal reign of Jesus, and the universal appeal of Jesus.*

Beyond this relationship of the kings of the east to king Jesus, I am intrigued with their relationship to King Herod. He was a sick-minded man, murdering most of those closest to him. He had his second wife killed, as well as her brother and her mother. Not to mention the slaughter of 45 leaders of the Jewish Sanhedrin early in his reign, and the murder of three of his sons, ordering the third killed only 5 days before his own death. It was of Herod that Caesar Augustus made the pun in Greek since the words were similar, that it was far better to be Herod's pig than his son—the pig had a better chance of surviving!

When Herod was troubled, that troubled the whole city of Jerusalem. No one knew what might happen in his rages. The strangers were seeking the one born king of the Jews. Now, nobody had been born king of the Jews for six centuries; certainly Herod had not been born to the throne. Like all dictators, he was constantly suspicious of all those around him. The scribes were glad to focus Herod's anger somewhere else, and Bethlehem seemed a likely target as they searched the Scriptures for the possible birthplace of the Messiah.

The scene in Matthew 2:7f had to be one of the most sacrilegious meetings ever to take place. Herod smoothly inquired exactly when they first saw the star, and they never guessed his real motive. He "learned of them carefully" (RSV) about the star, told them to go to Bethlehem, and requested them to kindly send word back to him when the child was found so he could also come and worship! As was said of General MacArthur, Herod never bowed down to anything but his mirror! When the kings left Herod, they went to Bethlehem. Since they found the Holy Family living in a house, the kings reached Bethlehem some time after Jesus' actual birth. In fact, when Herod sought to kill the Christ child, to make sure he caught the right child in his net he ordered all boy children under the age of two years to be slaughtered. The kings fell down and worshiped Jesus, and opened their gifts for him: gold, frankincense, and myrrh. They then went home "another way" rather than report to Herod.

The three kings disappear as quickly and totally from the Biblical scene as they came, but they leave in their wake all kinds of legends. Remember *"The Other Wise Man,"* by Henry Van Dyke? He speaks of another wise man, a fourth man, a fourth king from the east who was delayed in his rendezvous with the other three and thus did not travel to Judea to seek the king heralded by the star. Was there perhaps another king? Another king who should have knelt with the traditional three at the manger and opened gifts fit for a king? I think so; I truly think so. There is a missing king, one who has a basis in history and in fact. And I think that king was Herod! Herod is the missing king at the manger.

I realize there is much in Scripture which will never be completely clear to us, but I find only one good reason for the three kings to go to Jerusalem, to be led there by the star: to give Herod an opportunity to join them in worship of the Eternal king. It seems almost as if their stop at Jerusalem was guided by the Holy Spirit; not to get information—for they had the guiding star—but rather to give a message to Herod, an invitation to Herod, an opportunity to Herod, to join them in worshipping the newborn king. Let's not play Herod this Christmas, but rather join the Wise Men in seeking the newborn King.

The Dragon at the Stable

Matthew and Luke tell us of the events around the actual birth of Jesus—shepherds on hillsides, angels, starlight, Wise Men riding, Herod killing the boy babies, the Innkeeper and the manger. I think of their descriptions of the birth of Christ as *Christmas Card theology*. Delicate, emotional, beautiful, petite descriptions—just right for decorating Christmas cards. And if those beautiful pictures of the birth of Christ are as far as we go, then it is easy to keep Christ penned up between Thanksgiving and New Year! In John's Gospel our perspective is broadened, as he tells us that Jesus was in the Beginning...that everything was made by, for, and through Him. Here we also see the tragedy of Christmas: He came as a light in the darkness; He came unto His own, and His own received Him not!

Now see another account of Jesus' birth—one you may never have noticed! Turn to the twelfth chapter of Revelation, a book written in the midst of a demonic and broken world, in which only a minority believed in Jesus, written to a church facing persecution. See his account of Jesus' birth in verses 1-5. No shepherds dream here; no Wise Men march through this chapter; no Innkeeper offers even a stable for the Christ child. There is no light in the sky save the stars the dragon sweeps down. Here the close-up camera of Matthew and Luke has pulled back to take in all of God's drama of redemption. In Revelation we have the birth of Christ written in flaming scenes, with the whole sky as the stage.

What is the message of this Christmas story? Who is the woman in this picture? Who is the child? Who is the dragon? Are we in this story anywhere?

This Christmas story reminds us, in the first place, that God is faithful to His promises. Look at verses 1-5. The promises to David, to Abraham and to the prophets were not empty. The woman is, first of all, Old Testament Israel—the remnant; believing, faithful Israel; Chosen Ones from whom would come the Messiah. What a majestic figure she is! And the writer intended for the first readers of this book, and you today, to realize that God is faithful to His promises.

Secondly, the birth of Jesus set in motion an unearthly struggle between God and Satan. See verses 3-5, 7-9. Even in the Christmas Card theology of the Gospel accounts of Jesus' birth we see faintly that hideous strength—there is no room in the inn, and Herod tries to kill the babies. But this writer says that out in the dark just beyond the lamplight of the stable we can see—if we look closely—the blood-red eyes of the dragon. We can see the flickering tail that lashes down a third of the stars, we can see his heaving flanks and smell his foul breath. . . just beyond the circle of the light of the manger. There's more at the stable than "sweet little Jesus boy!"

Christmas thrusts us back to the reality of the devil! For the dragon at the stable is the devil. Look at verse 9 and see the names of the devil: the great dragon, the old serpent, the devil, satan, he who deceives the whole world. The Bible is saying that this evil one fights God —and God's people. The old serpent lures us with lusts, he is the deceiver and the accuser, always looking for our flaw, our weakness. Hear the truth of the Christmas carol:

> *God rest ye merry, Gentlemen,*
> *Let nothing you dismay,*
> *For Christ our Saviour was born*
> *on Christmas Day;*
> *To save our souls from Satan's power*
> *when we had gone astray.*

A Final Point: Christmas is not over yet! Look at verses 9-10, 17. *We are a part of the Christmas story!* He's talkin' about us! When the dragon couldn't kill the babe, he went after those he could reach—the child's family, people, church. He thought he could still nullify the cross and the resurrection toward which the stable is moving. The babe grew up, and twisted the defeat of the cross into victory. It is summed up in chapter 11, verse 15: "The kingdoms of this world have become the kingdoms of our Lord, and His Christ, and He shall reign for ever and ever."

If only our meditation upon that verse could bring us to the state of George Frederick Handel whose *Messiah*, written in 23 days during which he scarcely ate or slept, ends gloriously on that verse—a servant reported he saw Handel on his knees, tears streaming down his face, and he said, *"I did think I saw all heaven before me, and the great God Himself."*

May you see God this Christmas.

The Dullest Christmas Story Ever Told

Last Sunday was tough at the church where I am interim pastor. The whole congregation, it seemed to me, were asleep before I finished reading the scripture for the sermon! On the one hand, that's a compliment to the preacher, because it says they have confidence in his theology and don't have to keep an eye on him. On the other hand, it doesn't make the preacher feel very good. But, in this case, it was justified. For my sermon text, I read to the congregation the string of "begats" with which Matthew begins his Gospel. (Check out Matthew 1:1-17). You'd have gone to sleep too! There is nothing more boring than a genealogical list; a bunch of names—unless your name is in it.

But Matthew knows what he is doing. The Jews of Jesus' day put a lot of stock in genealogy. Some folks were very proud of the fact that they could actually trace their family back to David. The priests had to be able to prove descent from Aaron, and their wives must track their families back five generations. King Herod was sensitive to this love of genealogy, and since he was only one-half Jew, he made an effort to destroy the six great libraries of genealogy kept by the Sanhedrin. He failed. But Matthew is dealing with belief, not courthouse records.

Matthew begins his list of names by saying that Jesus is the son of David, the son of Abraham. He further divides the list into three groups of 14 generations. First, from Abraham to David, then from David to the Exile, then from the Exile to the birth of Jesus. His first point is that Jesus is the fulfillment of the promises to Abraham. The promises of God to Abraham were to be spiritually fulfilled, which ought to be clear when we realize Abraham never owned, in the Promised Land, anything but a cave in which to bury Sarah. It is through Jesus Christ, the son of David, the son of Abraham, that all the nations would be blessed, and through Him Abraham's children would be more numerous than the stars, or sand on the seashore.

Matthew also says Jesus is the son of David. He is the fulfillment of the promise to David that a descendant of his would always be on the throne. Yet David's kingdom is gone. But Jesus, the son of David (as well as son of Mary and son of God), rules forever.

And then there are those women. If you carefully study the list of names Matthew gives, you will see that he leaves out some kings, and adds in some women, like Tamar and Rahab and Bathsheba and Ruth. What a list—three of them have moral problems; all of them are non-Jews! Why on earth are they in a Jewish genealogy? Simply to say a couple of things: (1) Salvation is by grace! No list is ever made of righteous people; God can write straight with a crooked stick, and does so. There is no earning of salvation. (2) The Gospel is for all people everywhere, not just the "chosen" people. The list of names is not about genealogy; it is about the salvation that Matthew says has come to us in Jesus of Nazareth.

So, this Christmas season, "go tell it on the mountains, that Jesus Christ is born." And, if your pastor preaches on Matthew's genealogy, don't go to sleep—he just might have a great sermon!

The Jolly Season and Forgiveness

"'Tis the season to be jolly. . ." But a lot of folks are not jolly in this season. To be truly jolly and joyful in the Christmas season takes some preparation. It means we must again live in our own minds the enormity of what this season means. My experience is that a lot of people are locked up tight with materialism, depression and unforgiveness, which keeps them from experiencing the joy of the season.

Forgiveness and taking out the garbage are both unpopular, but if we do not tend to them, both quickly begin to stink to high heaven. And anyone who says it is easy to forgive has just never tried it. Why do you think we find it so hard to forgive? There are several aspects to unforgiveness, and one powerful blockage to forgiveness is that *we often don't want to forgive!* We don't want to let go of our bitterness, our hurt feelings, our desire for revenge. And that may mean that these emotions have fed upon us for so long that they have shaped our life and the kind of person we are. If we were to give up our sense of hatred, our enjoyment of our hurt and bitterness, we might not recognize the person in the mirror! That's a sobering thought; I don't want to be shaped by hatred and anger—do you?

Another reason we find forgiveness to be difficult is because we *often misunderstand what forgiveness actually is.* To forgive does not mean that we *agree* with what the person we are forgiving did to us. When God forgives us, it surely does not mean that He agrees with what we have done. Jesus did not approve of the conduct of the adulterous woman, but he forgave her. When we forgive someone, it is not an endorsement of their actions. Forgiveness does not mean approval of what has happened, nor does it mean *excusing what the person did.* We excuse a person when we feel they aren't to blame; but we forgive someone when we *do* feel they do have responsibility for what they have done.

There are lots of reasons why we must forgive others. For Christians, we must forgive because *a forgiving spirit is a mark of Christian legitimacy.* Look at Matthew 5:43f. We are admonished to be like our Heavenly Father. We are pointed to a lifestyle which is indeed different from this world. As Christians we remember the beau-

tiful story of Joseph in the Book of Genesis. One of the most moving passages is in the 44th chapter, when Joseph demands, as a test,
that the brothers leave behind in Egypt the youngest brother, Benjamin. Another brother, Judah, becomes a shadow of our Christian
stance when he says they simply cannot go home without Benjamin;
it would break the father's heart. *We cannot go home without our
brothers.* Christians must not let unforgiveness mar the pilgrim walk
together. Hubert Humphrey illustrated this truth majestically: on his
death bed Hubert Humphrey asked his longtime political foe, Richard Nixon, to sit beside his—Humphrey's—wife at Hubert's funeral.
His reason was simple: *"What I have concluded about life, when all
is said and done, is that we must forgive each other, and redeem each
other and move on."*

We remember the poet Edwin Markham especially for his little
poem about forgiveness:

> *He drew a circle that shut me out,*
> *Rebel, heretic, a thing to flout.*
> *But love and I had the wit to win—*
> *We drew a circle that took him in.*

What most do not know is that Markham wrote those words at
a hard time in his life. One he trusted had stolen all his savings.
He tried to write again to make a living, but found he was dry as a
rock. Finally he poured out his resentment to God and asked God to
cleanse his life and give him the power and grace to forgive. He did
forgive, and only then did he begin to write again. And these words
are among his best in these last years.

We're entering the season of Advent, the season that celebrates
the first—and the second—coming of Christ. What a shame not to be
able to taste eternity in the joy of these days! But to do so may mean
that you and I have to struggle, to fight, and to cast off the coils of an
unforgiving spirit. If we don't, our bitterness will shape us—not in
the image of Him whose birth we soon celebrate, but in the image of
one who is Christ's foe; one whose doom is certain and whose time

is short.

There's probably nothing more important for you to do this morning than to pray for a forgiving spirit, and then to go forth to put legs on your prayers.

A Most Unusual Shepherd

It was the stuff of stories. Stories that touch the heart at Christmas and let you know the real meaning of the season. We had gone back to make our yearly visit to our Memphis doctors, dentists, and to visit the church from which I retired. We have made it a habit to go during the December week that the church has the Alpine Village. I confess the Village was my brainstorm during a sleepless night. Other churches had their "Singing Christmas Tree" or something similar and I wanted us to do something as a church during the Christmas season to reach unchurched folks. I had this hunch that the singing tree brought in rural church members in the main, rather than unchurched people.

So the Village was born. Springing up in the church's gymnasium with an alpine theme, it included 11 small Swiss shopfronts, a 20-foot high working clocktower in the center, an area where it really "snowed" and the children could play in the snow, Santa Claus (and a note telling his true beginnings), a small chapel (seating about 10 people) in which the Gospel story was read, Alpen horns being played on the stage, a puppet show in the food court, and a goodie bag received at registration, in which to put your gifts. In each of the ten stores children could do an activity—make a photo Christmas card for the parents, build a toy, pick some candy, choose a Christmas book, decorate a gingerbread man cookie, make a Christmas ornament, etc. The gifts were all free, made by church members who worked all year to get the Village ready.

The first year we created the village we had 65 live Christmas trees decorating the area between the storefronts, 20,000 lights, popcorn carts, a town crier announcing the schedule of puppet shows and Alpen horn concerts, a toy train display, a bellchoir, and 3 kings who wandered in the crowd, asking where baby Jesus was to be found. (One little girl, on being asked by one of the kings where baby Jesus could be found, replied that he was over in Room 112!) She was referring to the room in which we had the nativity scene, completely with a baby Jesus which actually breathed, shepherds, and Mary and Joseph. We were worried about violating the fire code, but found that when the Fire Chief came over one night, all he wanted to know was the schedule—so he could bring his kids! The television stations gave free plugs for the Village.

That first Village drew 900 children and their parents. Each year the Village grows larger, with more and different shops and displays. Six years later, just before I retired, the village drew 2200 children plus their parents. We discovered that 20% of the Village visitors admitted on their registration form that they did not attend church anywhere. This past week as we visited the Village in its eleventh year, 2400 children had already pre-registered online ahead of the event, and 85 families wanted more information about the church. Some say the Village is a miracle.

But here's a real miracle. One of the precious families in that church was made up of dedicated parents and two children, a boy and a girl. The son has Down's Syndrome. The family was an inspiration as they cared for this son. Then about three years ago tragedy struck, and the wife suddenly died. The church family felt it was almost unfair for such to happen to this family whose faith was a blessing to all. Someone told of visiting the home shortly after the wife died and finding the son playing the piano. Asked about it, he replied that he was playing for his mother in heaven.

Well, Kyle, for that is his name, although he has Down's Syndrome, has a full and meaningful life. He is now working parttime at Chick-Fil-A, and does a great job cleaning up. Last week at the village I met him in the hallway and he excitedly told me of his new job. He also told me, with great pride, that he was a shepherd in the Nativity scene.

Later, as Pegeen and I started to leave, word came from the Nativity folks that Kyle wanted us to see him as a shepherd in the Nativity scene. So, the "angels" who kept the door and only allowed small groups to enter at a time, let just my wife and me enter the room. Beautifully lit, we saw the manger and the people. Folks are asked to enter and view the scene in silence, and so we quietly went in and stood before the tableau. Beside me was my wife, one beloved by all the folks in the church, one known for her sacrificial work for the church and for being a second mother to many.

It was a beautiful scene. But it passed into the realm of legend and almost brought us to tears when, in the silence of this reverent moment as we stood before the manger, one of the shepherds, Kyle, said to my wife in a soft whisper: "I love you."

It's that kind of love—non-judgmental, overflowing with depth— that brought the Creator of this world to wrap himself in human flesh and be born in a manger. "I love you."

Trouble at the Inn

Every Christmas I try to share the following story, written by Dina Donohue. It's the best nativity story outside the Bible that I know, and is a story that has become legendary. It can be found in the *Guideposts Christmas Treasury.* Listen to a paraphrase.

Wally was nine that year, and in the second grade, though he should have been in the fourth. Most folks knew that he had trouble keeping up. He was big and clumsy, slow in both movement and mind. Yet Wally was well liked by the other children in his class, all of whom were smaller than he. He was a helpful boy, cheerful, and a natural protector of the underdog.

Wally fancied the idea of being a shepherd with a flute in the Christmas play that year. But Miss Lumbard, the play's director, assigned to him a more important role. After all, she reasoned, the Innkeeper did not have too many lines, and Wally's size would make his refusal of lodging to Joseph and Mary all the more forceful.

And so it happened that the usual large, partisan audience gathered for the town's yearly extravaganza of bathrobed shepherds, coathanger-winged angels and squeaky voices. No one on stage or off was more caught up in the magic of the night than Wallace Purling. They said later that he stood in the wings and watched the performance with such fascination that from time to time Miss Lumbard had to make sure he didn't wander onstage before his cue.

Then the time came when Joseph appeared, slowly, tenderly guiding Mary to the door of the inn. Joseph knocked hard on the wooden door set into the painted backdrop. Wally the Innkeeper was there, waiting.

"What do you want?" Wally said, swinging the door open with a brusque gesture.

"We seek lodging."

"Seek it elsewhere." Wally looked straight ahead but spoke vigorously. "the inn is filled."

"Sir, we have asked everywhere in vain. We have traveled far and are very weary."

"There is no room in this inn for you." Wally looked properly stern.

"Please, good innkeeper, this is my wife, Mary. She is heavy with child and needs a place to rest. Surely you must have some small corner for her. She is so tired."

Now, for the first time, the Innkeeper relaxed his stiff stance and looked down at Mary. With that, there was a long pause, long enough to make the audience a bit tense with embarrassment.

"No! Begone!" the prompter whispered from the wings.

"No!" Wally repeated automatically. "Begone!"

Joseph sadly placed his arm around Mary and Mary laid her head upon her husband's shoulder and the two of them started to move away. The Innkeeper did not return inside his inn, however. Wally stood there in the doorway, watching the forlorn couple. His mouth was open, his brow creased with concern, his eyes filling unmistakably with tears.

And suddenly this Christmas pageant became different from all others.

"Don't go, Joseph," Wally called out. "Bring Mary back." And Wallace Purling's face grew into a bright smile. "You can have *my* room."

Some people in town thought that the pageant had been ruined. Yet there were others—many, many others—who considered it the most Christmas of all Christmas pageants they had ever seen.

And so do I. Merry Christmas!

A Father's Best Gift

So it's Father's Day again, and everybody forgot about it—but you! Well, don't fret about it. The important thing is that you leave to your children and grandchildren a heritage of which they can be proud. You know, most fathers are pretty good about making sure there is insurance to cover the wife and kids if anything [translate that: death] should happen to him.

But I've lived long enough to know some folks whose father left them a pile of money, but little else. You can turn money into groceries, but it doesn't turn into love, advice, understanding, or integrity. Did I ever tell you much about my father?

My Dad would be called an absentee father these days. You see, there were five boys and that meant he had to earn a living! He was an insurance man, back in the days when the insurance man had a route or "debit." He worked long hours, and often we children were in bed before he got home at night. He would go to the homes or businesses of his clients and collect the weekly premium for the insurance policy. He had both black and white customers. On Thursday afternoons, he "called the debit." That meant that one of us boys would call out the information on certain colored pages of his insurance book, while he added up the figures of the money collected.

But we did more than "call the debit." My father took us boys with him to pick figs at the yard of "Aunt Mary," an ancient black lady. He taught us the value of folks, regardless of the color of their skin. He took us fishing and hunting, too. (He could have used a bit more patience on fishing trips; but then several boys can hang up a lot of lines).

What I remember most about my father is not the money he left us—which wasn't that much—but odd little moments with each of us boys. I remember the day when he was taking me to school, and as we stopped at one of the three traffic lights in our burg, he placed his hand on my knee and told me that whatever I decided to become in life, he would see that the money for college was there. And he meant it. He himself had only an eleventh-grade education. After I felt called into the ministry, he often went with me to preach at little country churches as a senior in high school. I'm sure some of my sermonic disasters had to be embarrassing to him, but he had only encouragement.

I remember when he ran for sheriff of our county. My uncle had just finished serving 16 years, and the county wanted a change, so my Dad obviously didn't have a ghost of a chance. I was proud of his stand on moral issues, and his open letter to the citizens saying that if at any time while he was sheriff the local pastors of the First Baptist, First Methodist and First Presbyterian churches (that's the only churches in town) called together for his resignation, they would have it. He didn't win the election, and I still remember how we were at an uncle's service station listening to the returns; when it was obvious it was over, he simply said, "Let's go home, boys," and so we did.

My father was red-headed and was known as "Red," to everybody but his mother, whom I still remember calling him "Baby" when he was married and had us boys! He was outgoing with a sense of humor that was contagious. Everybody in our town and county knew "Red" Davis. And most loved him, and I still hear comments of appreciation whenever I go back to Madison.

But what I am most grateful for is the sense of right and wrong; the commitment to Christ and his Church; the basic integrity and honesty that my father passed on to his five boys. It was a powerful legacy, and the fact that four of the five boys earned doctorates reflects well on that heritage.

Well, Father's Day is here. Let's not worry about honors for ourselves, but reflect on the heritage we are passing on to our children and grandchildren. I think I hear a grandson wanting me to take him fishing.

New Year's and Goats

I know that January 1 doesn't really mark some deep change in the flow of the days of our lives. And yet, while there is no physical compartment we cross over at midnight on the 31st, the first day of the new year does indeed offer a powerful incentive for change, for a second chance. And who among us doesn't need a second chance! So, go ahead with those resolutions—no doubt you will break most of them before the end of January, but you'll not be any worse off than if you hadn't made the effort!

Over the holidays I read a most interesting book entitled *Last in Their Class: Custer, Pickett and the Goats of West Point* by James Robbins. It is a fascinating account of the careers of the West Point cadets who ended up at the bottom of their class at the academy. The man at the very bottom of the list was known as the "goat", a term denoting stubbornness, persistence, mischievousness and playfulness. And so they were. Apparently some cadets put more brain power and energy in reaching the objective of being the man at the bottom of the class than others put into being first in their class. The lowest academic group of cadets were known as the "Immortals." Based, I suppose, on the reality that even if some of those at the bottom failed, those who remained at the tail end of the class became the newest last section. So it was that the Immortals were always with the class.

The two most famous "goats" were George Custer and George Pickett. No, U.S. Grant was not at the bottom of his class as is often said; he was 37th out of 41 in his class—which in itself made him an "Immortal."

George Armstrong Custer was the goat of his class in 1861. But by the end of June in 1863 he was commissioned a brigadier general of volunteers, at that time the youngest American general officer in history at the age of 23. He went on to become a major general in the war years. Of course you know his end.

Another goat was George Pickett of the class of '45, who distinquished himself in the Mexican War, and went on to become a major general and division commander in Lee's army. In July of 1863 Pickett became a household name and achieved lasting fame with "Pickett's Charge" at Gettysburg.

The book is full of the amazing and brave exploits of these men at the bottom of the class. The "goats" of West Point in general were as brave and resourceful as the top men in their class in warfare.

Sometimes they just needed a second chance to prove themselves. As I read that very entertaining book, I began to think about how it is true in all of life—most of us need a second chance. Oftentimes a judgement based on one effort will not tell the whole story. Perhaps it is true in your life.

I'd hate to be judged by my high school or college record. And I think that, with a second effort, some crooked areas of my life could yet be straightened up. A second chance is invaluable. Ask the person who has managed to stop drinking, or kick the habit of smoking, or the one who made a terrible mistake and served jail time and now, years later, is an exemplary and productive citizen. Ask the one who responded to Christ in a Billy Graham crusade about what the second chance Christ offers has meant in his or her life.

That's what the New Year is for, I think. The opportunity to draw a line in the sand, to make some resolutions, to make some vows to God, to move from the "goat" to—perhaps—the hero.

You know, I ate everything that didn't eat me this holiday season. I guess now's the time to turn over a new leaf, to make some resolutions, to tighten the belt, to go on the diet . . . And you?

Calendars and Second Chances

Nothing actually changed last night at midnight, you know. For a calendar is an arbitrary milestone on the road of the years. While the Egyptians were the first to make calendars, the Romans influenced us to live by it. The Romans had a 10 month year, with March as the first month. Later, around 150 BC, the Romans added January and February and moved the beginning of the year to January. After all, January had to do with the festival of the god of the gate and so the year should begin there. But the Romans didn't have a good way to measure how long it takes this old ball to go around the sun, and it turned out their year wasn't quite right. So that, by the time of Julius Caesar, when it was autumn according to their calendar, it was summertime according to the facts! So Julius Caesar reformed the calendar, and when he re-lengthened the days and months, the calendar was only off 11 minutes and 45 seconds each year. That's nothing—we waste that much time every day!

But as the centuries rolled on, that 11 minutes and 45 seconds each year began to add up. And by the Middle Ages we were ten or twelve days out of sync! So Pope Gregory, in 1582, corrected the calendar by having folks go to bed one night—October 5—and wake up the next morning on October 15. Most folks grumbled and growled and went along with the Pope; but not the British! With their stiff upper lip, bulldog temperament—and especially since the Pope said do it—they just said, "Yes, well" and dragged their feet for 150 years. But in 1752 England finally went to the "new style" calendar and jumped from September 2 to September 14. It really created a lot of problems; workers in England demanded to be paid their wages for those missing days, and others resented being that much older. And in the middle of all that English changing, they decided to move the beginning of the year to January! Obviously the new year is a wandering designation. So what are we trying to say with the new year celebrations and resolutions?

First, *we are giving expression to a need we feel to stand back and examine and evaluate our lives.* Most things in life demand an evaluation; whether it's playing a piano, preaching a sermon, riding a bicycle or courting a girl, we ask ourself: *How am I doing?* I used to dream of a "no report card" school, but I realize some evaluation is needed along the way. Even our shadow is an evaluation of ourselves—it proclaims to the world whether we are tall or short, fat or skinny; and after stuffing during the holidays most of us shun our shadow!

Second, *we are saying we've failed in a lot of ways during the past twelve months, and we need a second chance.* I'm glad that along with the bent and grey old man with the sickle we see at this hingetime of the year, there's also the toddler wearing the new year sash! All of us goof up pretty miserably over the course of the year, and may God give us the grace to realize it and ask for a second chance. There's an old homespun poem that says it so well:

> He came to my desk with quivering lip;
> The lesson was done.
> "Dear teacher, I want a new leaf," he said
> "I've spoiled this one.
>
> I took the old leaf, stained and blotted
> And gave him a new one all unspotted;
> And then to his sad eyes I smiled,
> Do better now, my child.
>
> I went to the throne with a quivering soul;
> The old year was done.
> Dear Father, hast Thou a new leaf for me?
> I have spoiled this one.
>
> He took the old leaf, stained and blotted
> And gave me a new one all unspotted,
> And into my sad heart smiled,
> "Do better now, my child."

Third, *our marking of the new year is more than simply a time of evaluation, a time to face the realization of our mistakes; it is a time of optimism.* Every New Year's resolution says, "Give me another chance and I'll do better!" The reason Dickens' *A Christmas Carol* has touched hearts for over 150 years since Dickens wrote it is because it is a picture of hope for one who has failed miserably. Even Scrooge is given a second chance, and we are told he used it well. What will you do with your new chance?

Thoughts on Thanksgiving

Sometimes those articles on Thanksgiving get a soupy, I think. You know, while you're poised to carve a huge turkey you pause to consider our freedoms, etc. Not that I disagree with the sentiment; rather the opposite. I do think we need to pause and consider all our blessings. But I got to thinking about what I'm grateful for . . .

And looking out over the Yadkin valley I realized I'm really thankful for the natural beauty of our earth. And I begin to think about the kind of God who would create such beauty—golden and purple maples in autumn, snowflakes with the uniqueness of humans, tiny unbelieveably beautiful flowers heralding the coming of spring, dancing icy creeks and flashing trout—what kind of God would be interested in such things?

Sometimes we think God is a stern Judge, complete with long beard and frown. I rather think that if you must think of God in "grandfather" terms, we ought to see him with a face of sadness. Sad because of our rebellion and sad because of the way we have treated this magnificent creation. I'm not at all surprised that God came walking in the cool of the day in the garden he made for Adam and Eve. I wouldn't be surprised if God still comes strolling in the beauty of the forests and mountains and beaches that he has made for us to enjoy.

So, coupled with a strong sense of gratitude for this wonderful creation at this Thanksgiving time is a strong sense of our having made a mess of a creation of wonder. Granted, I didn't always give much thought to this business of ecology, this business of being good stewards of the earth. But, we should all grow up sometime, shouldn't we?

I haven't read Al Gore's book or seen his film, but whether or not you and I agree down the line with his "preaching" about ecology, we can agree that we have sinned against God in the way we desecrate his world. We have tended to see our world as here for us to abuse any way we wish to cater to our desires. Especially is this true in developed nations, and most especially is this true in America.

Sometimes it's a bother to recycle, to "take out everything you take in" to the backwoods and camping areas, but it's worth it in the long run. Our selfish and unthinking attitude is seen in the beer cans and bottles littering roadsides; the old fridge someone just pushed over the edge of the country lane; the adolescent urge we seem to have to drive vehicles which pollute and get low mileage per gallon; our insatiable hunger for more and more materialism which strips this world of resources and beauty.

This Thanksgiving, why not try to see this world *as God made it*—filled with a beauty that is fragile and at the mercy of you and me, we who are called to be the stewards of this magnificent creation. This Thanksgiving, why not try to see this world *as God sees it*—trampled upon and abused by his highest creation, human beings. Surely the heart of God is heavy at our selfishness and irresponsibility. Look no further for evidence of the sinful nature of us all. This Thanksgiving, why not try to see this world *as God wants it to be*—a tiny speck of beauty in the midst of a huge universe, peopled by folks who know him and love him, and want to take care of his world. Why not go out and pick up some trash alongside the highway!

The Three-Legged Stool of Marriage

The movie *"Message in a Bottle"*, which came out a few years ago, probably made more women cry and more men feel guilty than any movie in a long time. Teresa, the wife of Garrett, dies and Garrett is filled with loss and guilt. He writes a letter to his dead wife and puts it in a bottle which washes up on a shore. A beautiful single woman finds it and—but that's another story. In the letter Garrett shares what he wishes he had done—been more kind, apologized more, taken better care of her and so on.

Most men clearly know that feeling. Marriage is not easy. Most marriages seem not to have been made in heaven, but out of spare parts on the earth. And it takes a lot of effort to have a truly success-ful marriage. If I were to ask our readers to rate your marriage on a scale of one to 10, there would be a lot of low scores! But in addition to seeking the will of God through prayer, Christian friends and fol-lowing the admonitions of the Bible, there are three principles neces-sary for a happy marriage. Marriage is like a three-legged stool.

The first leg is *cooperation*. In Mark 10 Jesus speaks of God's intention in marriage, and says the man is to "cleave" to his wife (KJV). We think of "cleaving" or splitting wood. But the Greek word here means the opposite—being laminated, sticking together. Maybe the wedding ceremony ought to have both bride and groom say to each other: *"And I'm stuck with you as long as we both shall live!"* There has to be a sense of unity in the couple's dreams and hopes. A willingness to give in, to give over, to make the common dream work.

The second leg on this stool of marriage is *communication.* Marriages don't just fall apart overnight. Usually it is the result of a growing distance between the couple. The man was kidding himself when, after watching his hair fall out for years, he suddenly looked in the mirror after the last hair fell out, and declared, "Great scott, I'm bald!" He had been in the process a long time! Communication in word and deed is essential for a good marriage. Talk about the prob-lems. But—don't get *historical.* That is, don't bring up everything your spouse has ever done wrong. Stick with the present issue. And remember, even John Wesley's wife used to sit in the congregation and stick out her tongue at him—there is no perfect marriage! Work on it!

The third leg is that of *consecration.* Marriage is God's idea; God's wonderful gift to us. Genesis tells us that God paused in the processes of creation to say, "It is good!" The only thing that wasn't good was the fact that man was alone. So God made a "helpmeet", a partner with whom Adam could experience the spiritual nature of life more fully. A family relationship to God is essential for a marriage as God intends it. It's like a wagon wheel; as the spokes get closer to the hub, they get closer to each other.

In the merry month of May, when springtime dresses the hills, when a young man's fancy turns to a beautiful girl, think on these things!

Your Second Most Important Decision

It's June. Time for heat waves, bugs and—traditionally—weddings. But seems folks get married just about any old time these days. The important thing is probably not whether you get married in June or October, but whether you hold a high view of marriage. I think the decision to marry someone is the second most important decision you will ever make, second only to the decision to follow Christ as Lord of your life.

Yet marriage is a battered institution as we march into the 21st century. Sitcoms, movies and novels both create and reflect the attitude that living together before marriage and divorce after marriage is the assumed practice. I dare say there is less fulfillment, not more, in people's lives since the value of marriage went down. In case you're among those who still believe that marriage is a divine institution and that the deepest joys of life are bound up with marriage, let me say a word about strengthening your marriage. Make a note, please, that this is a report from the trenches; that after 47 years of marriage, I still don't know much about women, and am certainly not a model husband. (But I try.)

The idea of emphasizing freedom, separate goals and separate careers in marriage has taken a terrible toll. Hear me out; I have no problem with women having careers or with men doing chores around the house and changing diapers. But I am saying that when you enter into the relationship of marriage, it has to take precedence over individual agendas.

As an example, take the case of the young couple who came to the pastor just days before the weddding, all upset and unsure about going through with the event. The problem turned out to be where to go on the honeymoon. It was a winter wedding, and the groom wanted to have a "hunting" honeymoon out west. He wanted his bride to spend the days in a cold, damp hunting blind with him. She, on the other hand, had definite ideas about the honeymoon—New York with its stage shows, operas, fine restaurants and such.

Hiding his amazement at such immaturity as this fuss, the pastor suggested a solution. The bride should be agreeable to the hunting expedition. But she should take along her CD player, and while they were waiting for the trophy elk, she could play Mozart or Brahms or whomever, as loud as she wished. And, turn about being fair play, since the groom griped that she always wanted him to go to the opera with her, he must do that. But, he could take his hunting rifle and bag a cellist or flutist or such. The absurdity of the situation struck home, and couple realized concessions are a part of marriage. No man, or woman, should enter into the new relationship of marriage unless it takes precedence over previous relationships. Marriage must be on the front burner, and it is a continuing adjustment, a life-long learning process.

Now, don't kid yourself; all marriages have fusses and spats. Three ladies were talking. Said the first: We've never had a harsh word in our marriage. Later said the second: I wish we could say that! Replied the third lady "why not? She did!" Men and women are different, and there will be disagreements in a healthy marriage. W.C. Fields put it dryly when he said, upon being asked if he believed in clubs for women: "Yes, if all other means of persuasion fail!" A pastor asked one woman who came in for counseling in her marriage how she handled her obvious hostility toward her husband; said she: "After he leaves for work I swish his toothbrush around in the toilet bowl for awhile." There has to be a better way to deal with problems!

There is some incompatibility in each marriage. Ogden Nash had something when he said, "I believe a little incompatibility is the spice of life; particularly if he has income and she is pattable!" Yet how tragic when husband and wife pass like ships in the night; communication totally lost between them. John Milton once replied to a man who said his (Milton's) wife was a rose: "She may be; I certainly feel the thorns!"

Most marriages would deepen and prosper if one thing were done: if the marriage was centered around the community of faith. There is a deep religious aspect to marriage which is often forgotten, yet it is the cement of the relationship. If our marriage is a special creation of God, then we have a responsibility to tend, nurture and strengthen, and not destroy it. When we treat the institution of marriage as a temporary thing; when we put ourselves first instead of our spouse, we are crippling a wonderful, fulfilling experience. God knew what he was doing when he instituted marriage. There's no doubt, however, that his idea runs counter to our society. Ours is an age of "throw away." We think in terms of a short lifespan of a car, a stove, and even a marriage.

On Babies

Well, we just got word about 15 minutes ago that we are grandparents again! In a way that's nothing new, since this is our sixth, and probably last, grandchild. We're told she is a little doll, and naturally we believe that. Never mind that all the new babies I've ever seen looked just like Winston Churchill without his cigar!

However, you never forget the sight of your firstborn. I was in seminary here in North Carolina, and my wife worked with the Baptist State Convention. Our son was born in Rex Hospital in Raleigh, and my main memory of that hospital was that in the lobby there was a statue of Christ. Good for starters, but most all the fingers on the statue were broken off. I remember thinking that he was reaching for us, but couldn't quite make it. It's odd the things brand-new fathers think of! I'm sure the statue has been replaced now.

We had been so excited over this child that we would have thought him a handsome fellow no matter what he actually looked like. I fully realized what he looked like only on the evening of his birth. That morning I was on a high, as all new fathers are. I went back to the seminary for classes, and came back that evening with my best friend. I had been bubbling over with vivid descriptions of my fine son. And then finally my friend and I were standing in front of the glass wall there in the maturnity ward, staring in at all the babies in their cribs, complete with the last name on the sign on the crib. At first I thought maybe there was a mistake. But, no, the sign said "Baby Davis" in bold letters. My friend simply looked over at me with the wisdom and pity that a 22-year-old bachelor has. I shrugged and admitted that this child, my son, did indeed look like a dried up little monkey! He only weighed 5 pounds, 4 ounces, and appeared to be slipping out of one leg of his diaper! Well, to make that story short, he turned out to be a fine man, and he and his wife have made us proud, with first a set of twins, and now a beautiful granddaughter.

Funny how love transforms everything, isn't it! But what an awesome responsibility it is to bring a child into this world. I am concerned as I watch modern parents. While there are still plenty of wonderful parents, I perceive that many children will not have a foundation of a solid home, with two parents who truly love God, love one another and love the child. I see children without a moral foundation, because too many well-meaning parents refuse to impart moral values, saying the child should choose their own religion, choose their own moral values.

Yet for all that talk, children's lives are shaped by the values they see in those adults around them. And here I ought to say, "God bless schoolteachers!" There is no doubt that my schoolteachers had as much shaping influence on me as did my parents. After all, I was with the teacher more waking hours than with my parents. And our schoolteachers have the high privilege of shaping the morality, the values, the world outlook of many children.

And the church. Funny how we often end up searching for warm bodies to serve as teachers of our Sunday School program, not realizing the great opportunities and responsibility they have. Put your best teachers in the classes of the young children. My earliest memory of church is that of a flower, with the face of my Beginner teacher superimposed in that flower. Some of my Sunday School teachers shaped my religious thinking in a way that inspires me 65 years later.

So, fellow grandparents, raise a cup—or say a prayer—for my new granddaughter. Ah, she's a bonnie lass! And, why not talk with your pastor about teaching in the nursery or young children's area in your church. The dividends are out of this world!

Patriotism

It seems to me that a person has a sense of patriotism either because they came from an experience where they were not free—i.e, they stood on the deck of a ship and saw the lady with the lamp in the light of the dawning of a new day for them—or else, like most of us, we were born free. In both cases we need to be reminded every so often of freedom, of its cost, and of the place of our nation under God. So indulge my wandering thoughts.

My sense of patriotism was nurtured by two incidents in my

childhood in north Florida. First was the yearly march out to the cemetery to stand by the Confederate graves, all 21 of them, and hear the account of the brave boys in grey. Although the nearest Civil War battle was really only a skirmish at Olustee, some 50 miles from Madison, as a child I figured it was a major battle! Some of the injured were brought to a genuine antebellum mansion in our town which was used as a hospital. And indeed, some years ago while vacationing in New England, in the midst of a small village I came to a monument around which the traffic went. As I went by, something caught my eye, and I went back to look. Yep, sure enough, here was a monument in Yankeeland to soldiers who had fought in the battle of Olustee. I know it's a certain kind of patriotism we Rebs have when we talk about the "War", but it's American patriotism, nevertheless.

The other incident which shaped my thinking on patriotism has to do with the Second World War and Captain Colin P. Kelly. Kelly was a native of our small town—population 3,000—and a graduate of West Point. On the day after Pearl Harbor, he and his B-17 crew bombed what they thought was a major Japanese carrier, and on the return the plane crashed. The rest of the crew escaped while Kelly tried to bring the damaged craft back to the field. President Roosevelt awarded Kelly the Medal of Honor, the first given in WWII. Kelly's portrait hung just inside the entrance of my high school, and the beautiful statue of the four angels of freedom, a tribute from the nation, stands on the edge of the city's park. Every day during my high school years I walked past that statue, always reading its inscription. When the war was over, the remains of Kelly were returned to Madison. I suppose I was in the second grade when they had the grand funeral. The flag-covered coffin was set in the rotunda of our courthouse, with an honor guard and all four doors to the courthouse opened so folks could look right in at the sight. I still remember how proud we all were of our hero, Captain Kelly.

I'm a patriot. Down to the marrow. And I'm glad I live in America. True, we have some sorry politicians, and although democracy is a poor way to do government judging by the fraud and graft, it's the best system on the face of the earth. I suppose my only hesitation about the Fourth of July is the way we want to mix patriotism and Christian faith. It took me a while to realize it, but America is not a Christian nation. We are not God's nation. God doesn't have a nation—He has a kingdom, and it is made up of people from every nation under the sun. And the god on our coins and the god our politicians so often refer to is not the father of the Lord Jesus Christ. The god we hear about in politics does not have the power to judge America—only the power to bless whatever our country does. That god is not the God of the Bible. And it bothers me to see us mixing religion and patriotism. God is above this or any nation. And to be a patriot is not the same as being a Christian. At the risk of sounding like the Old Testament prophets, I say we all need to begin to realize that God does not love this nation above other nations; nor has he blessed this nation in order for us to lavish wealth on ourselves. We have a duty to be a blessing to the rest of the world. I shudder when I hear ads on TV about treating our dog's stiff hips and putting our cat on a diet—when hundreds of thousands of human beings will go to bed hungry tonight and will starve before the year is out. Let us think on these things. God bless America! . . . God judge America too! and . . . God wake America up!

Thoughts on True Freedom

I suppose there is no greater symbol of freedom in the world than the Statue of Liberty. It is the symbol of a dream for most of the world; it is a symbol of a reality for us Americans. Engraved on the base of the statue are lines from Emma Lazarus' poem:

> Give me your tired, your poor,
> Your huddled masses yearning to breathe free,

The wretched refuse of your teeming shore,
Send these, the homeless, tempest-tost to me,
I lift my lamp beside the golden door.

Most of us were born free—We have never known anything else. We do not even understand that craving for freedom that haunts most of the world. I can remember vaguely the end of the Second World War, and how our class of first graders marched around the classroom with little American flags. I grew up taking freedom for granted. I never think of my elementary school days without calling to mind the beautiful young teacher—she broke all the boys' hearts by getting married at the end of that school year—blowing gently on her pitch-pipe and having the class sing during our music time such songs as

My country, 'tis of thee, Sweet land of Liberty, Of thee I sing;
Land where my fathers died, Land of the pilgrims' pride,
From every mountain side, Let freedom ring!

I cannot imagine being unjustly imprisoned; I cannot imagine my liberty being taken away when I have committed no crime nor broken any laws. My whole mindset about America, and freedom, and justice came from being under the stern gaze of George Washington and Abraham Lincoln, watching over us from their perch above the blackboard in my elementary school. My little hometown has the honor of being the home of America's first hero of World War II, Captain Colin P. Kelly, about whom I have already spoken. The nation put a beautiful monument in the town park, showing four angels, each representing one of President Franklin D. Roosevelt's "Four Freedoms" speech—freedom of speech, freedom from fear, freedom from hunger, and freedom of religion.

As I have grown older, I have come to realize that this mindset I grew up with is fast evaporating. We no longer have a clear vision about freedom, or a clear set of core values such as those we embraced as schoolchildren when we read from the Bible each morning at school, bowed our heads and prayed the Lord's Prayer, and then pledged allegiance to the flag and sang "My Country, 'Tis of Thee."

We have traded those values in for a pottage of diversity. And when nothing but our differences, our diversity, holds us together, we shall have no dreams, no freedoms, no future.

I have come to realize that freedom is not free. For more than two centuries, the price of vigilance has been paid in lives of young men and women in uniform. I am grateful. I have also come to realize that men cannot truly be free without God. Oh, I know that many folks—more than in my father's and grandfather's time—say that what we need in America is freedom *from* religion; freedom from God.

Can a man be truly free without God? A man will worship; that I know. If he laughs at God, he will worship money, or fame, or some person or some cause, or even himself. *Man was not made to try to live in isolation from God.* Nor yet was man made to create a god after his own image to worship. Unfortunately, in our time we have seen in our nation a growing tendency to create our own god who will serve our nation only, right or wrong. It is a tendency that is entwined in many churches as we mix patriotism and Christianity. But God has no nation. He has a kingdom, and people from every nation on earth are a part of that kingdom. God holds nations accountable.

As an observer—not an impartial one, mind you—of our culture for nearly 70 years, I have come to see that men are only truly free when they give up their spiritual independence, and depend on God. Let us not try to domesticate God, nor make Him in our image. Let us not seek to make God be on our side; let us determine to be on God's side.

So, unfurl the flag this weekend; go to church and thank God for His blessings on this nation. And ask Him to forgive us for trying to use Him so often for our personal and national goals. Pray that we might draw near to Him who is our strength.

A Short Primer on Patriotism

You never know when to celebrate July 4 when it comes in the middle of the week! Churches especially have a hard time deciding which weekend is the patriotic weekend. Perhaps as churches and Christians we ought to back off and consider the whole matter dispassionately. Let me lay out a brief primer on patriotism. Perhaps we will not all agree. But, Nathan, that's what sells newspapers—differences of opinion!

Point One: I am a patriot. I point this out by way of clearing out the underbrush. I've told you about my growing up in the small town (3,000 pop.) from which came the first WWII winner of the Medal of Honor, Captain Colin P. Kelly. I walked by his monument on the town square at least once a day. My school days were dominated by Abraham Lincoln peering down at me from above the blackboard. And yes, I made a makeshift Confederate flag and hung it above my bed. —But I don't have a Rebel flag symbol on my car. All of which is to say that if you want to have a July 4th Patriotic parade, I'm all for it, even on Sunday afternoon.

Point Two: Even though the water is muddy, we all ought to pray for the safe return of our soldiers. (We ought also pray for the enemy combatants and the innocent civilians who suffer the most in war). World War II was the last clear-cut, morally black-and-white war. One could wish these days that the issues were as clear and simple as they were in that war. There was literally almost no dissent at all; the entire country was ready to do whatever to stamp out the scourge of Hitler. Today it is not so clear, for the common citizen or for the congress, which makes the sacrifices all the more tragic. Yet we certainly pray for the cessation of bloodshed, and we fervently pray for the safe return of loved ones.

Point Three: As a Christian I love America and cherish the freedoms I enjoy here, while remembering that I have a higher allegiance. I am first and foremost a Christian. As a Christian my highest loyalty and allegiance belongs to Christ. I give to Caesar what is his—my taxes, my involvement as a citizen, my defence of freedom—but I give my soul, my integrity, my highest obedience to my Lord Jesus, the son of the only and living God. That does not mean I am not a good citizen, it simply means that I do not confuse patriotism and religion. And that leads to the next affirmation.

Point Four: I do not confuse Christianity and patriotism. In my judgement, one of the tragedies of recent decades is the merging of church and state. And, to the shame of the church, in too many cases from the pulpits themselves come the co-mingling of patriotism and Christianity. You respond that we are a Christian nation. What do you mean by that term? If you mean that the founders of this great country were Christians, you are in large part mistaken. If you mean that the rank and file, the common man in the 1700s and 1800s, was either a Christian or haunted by the Bible and its values, you are largely correct. On the frontier the home usually had two books, if no more: the Bible and Bunyan's Pilgrim's Progress. So our moral foundation is indeed the Bible. But you see, God does not have a nation; He has a kingdom. And people from every tribe and nation, every culture and tongue, can belong to that kingdom. But to say that America is special in the eyes of God is to twist the Biblical teaching of the prophets and Jesus. God is above all nations. God judges all nations. God honors those who keep His commandments. (We certainly cannot say we are a Christian nation in that sense). So, it behooves us to keep our genuine celebration of patriotism, and our clear understanding that God is not a dog on America's leash, as separate and powerful ideas. And that is why I am not in favor of turning any worship seervice into a patriotic rally. We come to church to worship Almighty God. Obviously it is certainly appropriate, on the July 4th weekend and any other time, to offer thanksgiving for our blessings, to confess our national sins, to ask for forgiveness for our pride, our selfishness in light of the starving nations, and to ask God to open all our eyes and hearts so we may be used to bless a world less fortunate. And then let's plan a patriotic parade at another time rather than in a worship service of God.

Point Five: Dealing with that old saying. There is an old pariotic saying I ought to leave with you. We've all heard, "My country, right or wrong." And believe it or not, some folks are morally bankrupt enough, or have so intertwined patriotism and Christianity, that they honestly think that is a fine saying, a good motto for these days. That's certainly not true as the saying stands. But I rather like what Carl Schurz, a German immigrant who was appointed by Abraham Lincoln as Ambassador to Spain and declined so he could serve in the War, who rose to the rank of major general on the wrong side of the Civil War and commanded at the battles of Bull Run, Chancellorsville and Gettysburg, who served in the cabinet of President Rutherford Hayes, and was a leading newspaperman, said about that proverb, "My country, right or wrong." *"The Senator from Wisconsin cannot frighten me by exclaiming, "My country, right or wrong." In one sense I say so too. My country; and my country is the great American Republic. My country, right or wrong; if right, to be kept right; and if wrong, to be set right."* A great statement; no idolatry of nation, yet strong love.

And I close with this wry comment on that old saying, "My country, right or wrong." *"My country, right or wrong' is a thing no patriot would ever think of saying except in a desperate case. It is like saying 'My mother, drunk or sober."* That is an assessment by the famous English writer, G. K. Chesterton.

Have a great holiday; celebrate your country, and worship your God.

Chapter Four

Reflections on Biblical Texts

Christ Without a Bucket

The old house is gone; a double-wide sits there now. The well behind it has been filled in; it used to be a long walk from the house, but now it is only 25 yards or so. My grandparents' farm and the old well are but memories now, but my, what memories linger there. I can still hear the clanking of the bucket as we let the rope sizzle down through the pulley, the bucket bouncing off the wall of the well as it descended. Then, finally, a splash and we knew the bucket was floating on the water. A flip or two of the rope and the bucket turned on its side and quickly filled. Now the groaning of the pulley as we hauled the bucket of water back to the top of the well. How I remember the metallic taste as we tilted the bucket and drank with our lips on the metal, and the cool water spilling all over us!

The Bible has an intriguing bucket story, you know. In the fourth chapter of the Fourth Gospel, a Christ who *must* go through Samaria stops wearily at Jacob's well and sends his disciples on into town. And then she comes, in the heat of the day, alone, an outcast woman, to draw her water apart from the sunset chatter of the village women as they come at the usual time to draw water.

He asks her for a drink. To give it the biblical twist, we must read it like this, as if it were still in the 1950's: "He asked her for a drink. She said, how come you, a white man, ask me, a black woman, for a drink? You know that blacks and whites don't even speak, much less a white man asking a black woman for a drink!"

His answer: "If you only knew who I am, and the gift of salvation, you would ask me to give you a drink of living water!" The saucy woman looks around, looks behind Jesus, peers down into the well, and makes her cynical reply: "This well is deep, and I don't see you carrying no rope and bucket! Just what are you going to use to get that water?" But Jesus isn't talking about the old oaken bucket, and she knows it.

They converse for awhile, and he asks her to go get her husband and come back; he wants to talk to them both. She looks down over the lip of the well, her loose hair hanging like a curtain around her face as she confesses: she has no husband. "Yes, he says, you have had five husbands, and the man you've shacked up with is certainly not your husband!" She hurries on over that comment to talk about religion—it's the one topic everybody knows all about. As soon as she can, though, forgetting her water jug, she hurries off into the village to tell them about a man who told her "everything that ever I did!"

And so they came. White robes coming through the fields to see this thing that had come to pass. A spiritual harvest already, even though it was four months til the wheat harvest. Such is the story, but for years I have gotten hung up on the question of the saucy lady: "The well is deep; where is your bucket?" What an odd image: Christ without a bucket!

Some wise person said salvation is free; but you have to have a bucket to carry it in. And that is so. There has to be bucket; a channel for the living water; a method to connect the grace of God on one hand with the need of the sinner on the other. As I have pondered that story of the woman at the well, I see Jesus using several spiritual buckets to deliver the living water to this woman and this village. There was the bucket of her *curiosity*. Curiosity killed the cat, but in so many cases it has brought new life. Zaccheus didn't just go out and climb a tree every morning before breakfast! It was curiosity that put him up a tree that day when Jesus passed by and changed a tax collector's life. And ponder the thousands upon thousands who went to a Billy Graham crusade out of curiosity and stayed to find the living water.

The woman at the well certainly was in a *crisis*, and it became a bucket to deliver the Gospel water. Her world had fallen apart; an outcast who went from man to man, never finding the love she needed. You may have first tasted the living water in the midst of a crisis of illness, of tragedy, of broken dreams; certainly you know of several folks who did.

But you know, I'm convinced the most effective bucket Jesus uses today to bring the life-giving water to guilty, thirsty sinners is the church. Perhaps I should close with a question to you who are churchgoers: *Have you ever reflected on how many ways your church is being used as a bucket to deliver the living water?*

I hear faintly a beautiful spiritual song: *"Fill my cup, Lord; I lift it up, Lord; come and quench this thirsting of my soul."* Somewhere, in your neighborhood, there is a woman—or a man—at the well, alone, outcast, out of hope, lifting a cup and seeking the living water. Go take it to them.

Goading a Man into Heaven: Acts 26

I've got some friends I'd like to see come to a personal commitment to the Lordship of Jesus Christ. As I reflect on how that might happen, I realize that my hammering on them won't cause them to come to Christ. I find that when a person becomes a Christian, it is due to several factors that all work together. Often we talk about Paul's miraculous, instantaneous conversion on the road to Damascus. Well, it wasn't. Nobody's is. I remember Martin, a man in my seminary church who was the typical unbeliever, the village atheist.

In fact, he had been known to throw garden produce at folks who came by to invite him to church! Well, he got deathly ill, and his entire view of life changed. In the months that remained to him, he couldn't give away enough garden vegetables; he couldn't express often enough how he had come to find Jesus in his illness, which was a goad, prodding him to salvation. *Nobody is converted in a vacuum.*

Think about the apostle Paul's conversion. In Acts 22:7 where Paul is arrested in Jerusalem and addresses the crowd, and again in Acts 26:14 where Paul is defending himself before Agrippa, he says the heavenly voice commented, *"it is hard for you to kick against the goads."*

It's an interesting image. Most of us have no experience with the lumbering old oxcarts and drivers who punched the oxen with long, iron-tipped spears to make them go in the right path. But Paul had seen that scene over and over; the stubborn animal refusing to go where the master planned for him to go. What Paul is saying is that God had been prodding him toward salvation, pushing him toward heaven, as it were, and he had been acting like a stubborn ox. Could the same thing have happened, or be happening, in your life? For Paul, the goads toward the Christian experience were fourfold. They may ring a bell in your life.

First, he was dealing with the *failure of his present religion.* He had spent most of his life trying to be good enough, work hard enough, to earn God's love. (Just like some children have to earn their parents' love). Yet he was more and more dissatisfied! Another goad was the *facts of the Christian faith.* We need to remember Paul wasn't watching the current religious scene in his day from the sidelines. He was involved in a big way! Had he seen and heard Jesus? We don't know how well Paul knew Jesus, if he had met him at all. Surely Paul was there at the trial of Jesus, and saw the calm assurance of the prisoner in the face of the ridicule and the false witnesses. And after the resurrection Paul surely had listened to Gamaliel's speech to the Sanhedrin (Acts 5:39) in which that great teacher had warned that if God was in the young Christian movement, the Sanhedrin would be found to be fighting God by persecuting the Christians. So Paul began to think, *"Am I fighting God?"* Could I be wrong about the scriptures, about the Messiah?

The third prod goading Paul to faith in Jesus was the *witness of the Christians.* These were unlearned, uneducated men, yet they spoke with a glad boldness about Jesus, and how he had changed their lives. They could not be frightened into silence or submission; they would not go quietly back to their fishing boats, even though Paul and others knew this man Jesus was dead. In fact, the more Paul stamped out this fire, the faster and bigger it grew! The Christian movement seemed like these trick birthday cake candle flames that keep coming back, no matter how hard you blow them out. I think what got to Paul was their joyful commitment to what they believed. He simply didn't have that.

And the fourth prod God used on Paul was his *sense of sin and guilt*, especially concerning Stephen. You see, while Paul didn't actually throw stones at Stephen, he certainly was an accessory to the murder. He held the coats of those who did throw the rocks; and holding the coats was a sort of honorary position of involvement and encouragement. Can you imagine standing there while the men whose coats you hold actually bash in the head of Stephen with rocks? Paul never quite got away from the horror of what he did on that day, nor could he submerge Stephen's words of confidence and faith and forgiveness.

But finally it all caught up with Paul. On his way to even greater success as a crusading pharisee, armed with the encouragement of Judaism's finest, he set out for Damascus. And then it all came together at some forgotten place on that road: *the failure of his old religion, the unanswered facts about Jesus, the shining testimony of the saints, and the guilt about Stephen.* Paul collapsed and Jesus picked him up. Paul was finally prodded into the kingdom. But it wasn't easy; even Jesus said to Paul, *"It's hard to kick against the prods, Paul."*

It's something to think about. In spite of all your questions about the faith, and in spite of all the hypocrites in the church. And it may be why your side is so sore! Those goads sure do sting!

He Asked Him About His Disciples: John 18

The Lenten season is a march toward the cross; a time of introspection, of asking, "Is it I, Lord?" A while back I was studying the story of Jesus' betrayal and comparing the four Gospels. If you turn to the Gospel of John, to chapter 18 where we are told of Jesus' arrest in the garden, his interrogation by the high priest, the flight of the disciples and the denials of Simon Peter, you will perhaps notice a striking situation.

Notice that the writer emphasizes the disciples in this chapter. They are mentioned twice in the first verse. Judas knows where Jesus is, because Jesus often went to that garden to pray with his disciples. Judas comes with the soldiers to arrest Jesus—indeed, we are told that "Judas was standing with them"—in more ways than one. When Jesus is arrested, he asks that his disciples be allowed to go free. Yet Simon slashes a servant's ear.

Next, the soldiers take Jesus to the high priest, or rather to Annas, the father-in-law of Caiaphas, who was the high priest that year. After setting the scene in the high priest's house, the writer takes us outside into the courtyard, where Peter and another disciple have gained entrance. Peter is recognized by a servant girl and denies any knowledge of Jesus. We are told it is cold and he stands around a fire warming himself.

Punch pause on the video in your mind, and realize that the writer of this Gospel now takes us back inside where the questioning of Jesus is taking place. Verse 19 tells us that the high priest "questioned Jesus about his disciples and his teaching." Oddly, Jesus does not respond to the question about his disciples, but speaks of his doctrine.

His answer is not pleasing, a soldier slaps him, and the writer takes us back outside.

Verse 25 picks up the thread of Peter's denials. The same phrase ending verse 18 is picked up here: Peter stood warming himself at the fire. Is the Gospel writer simply moving back and forth between the interrogation of Jesus and the denials of Peter in a random fashion, or is he telling us something. (Don't get sidetracked here; the Holy Spirit inspired the writers, yet allowed their own thoughts to be a part of the divine narrative).

Imagine the scene inside the high priest's home: the high priest is pleased to get what is perhaps his first actual sight of Jesus, the troublemaker from Galilee. He's heard of some of Jesus' teaching—"Blessed are the meek, etc. etc." "Not bad stuff; but what about these disciples? Are they just good ol' boys, well-meaning but misled, or are they genuine troublemakers for Rome, and therefore for the religious hierarchy? After all, didn't one of your men, Peter they call him, cut off one of my servants' ears this very night?"

Now look at the text again and you will see that Jesus didn't respond to the question about his disciples. He doesn't need to, because the Gospel writer answers the question for Jesus! The writer breaks into the description of Peter's denials and inserts this question and the lack of an answer on Jesus' part—answering the question in the very writing of the Gospel account!

Reflection on this scripture will likely lead us to conclude that Jesus said nothing to Annas about his disciples for two reasons: first, in order to protect them. If the high priest were to dwell on the Twelve (eleven now), he might well decide that it is as easy to nail up eleven as it is to nail up one. Second, there wasn't a great deal Jesus could say about them at that moment, was there?

But let us not be too hard on Peter at this point. Sure, he did deny Christ. But exactly what did he deny? Not the virgin birth, not the divinity of Jesus, not the miracles, not the second coming. He denied none of the things that we so often get so worked up about and divide churches and denominations. He simply said he didn't know the man. Now there's where the water hits the wheel. Who isn't guilty of living in ways that deny we ever knew Jesus! I suspect that most of the AIG executives and others receiving bonuses on backs of the poor are church members; folks who would be orthodox in belief, regular in church attendance . . . but obviously live as if they never knew Him. But don't dwell on them, but on ourselves. Do you and I live daily in such a fashion that folks will know by our compassion for others that we are disciples of Jesus?

"He asked him about his disciples." I sure hope nobody is down at the corner cafe asking about me; about whether I am a disciple of Jesus. Maybe these days when we are relentlessly marching toward the cross and the resurrection ought to truly be a time of soul-searching.

Mark's Portrait of Jesus

The other day a fellow asked me a question that had been bothering him: "Pastor, how come Luke's Christmas story has those Wise Men, and Mark's Gospel doesn't?" Well, I had to deal with two aspects of his question! First, I told him, Luke's Gospel doesn't have those Wise Men! That's in Matthew's Gospel. And as for Mark not having them, that opens up a whole new can of worms—or at least a new learning opportunity.

Let me take a few moments to acquaint you with the Gospel of Mark. I know, I know, you are thoroughly familiar with Mark's Gospel. But would it be all right if we act as if we knew nothing about Mark? Good. Let's begin by realizing that Mark's Gospel is the first one written. That's right; almost all scholars think that Mark wrote the first Gospel to be written.

Then why is Matthew's Gospel first in the New Testament? Well, it's like this. For perhaps 1700 years, everyone thought Matthew's Gospel was written first, and that Mark's Gospel was just a summary of Matthew. In the last century or so, it has become evident that Mark is the earliest Gospel. About 90% of Mark's Gospel is found in Matthew and Luke, in the same word order. It seems quite clear that the other Gospels copied Mark and added to it. And, I might add lest I be misunderstood, the differences in the Gospels were guided and inspired by the Spirit of God.

Take a look with me at the Gospel of Mark. Half of it deals with the last week in the ministry of Jesus. So it is obviously not intended to be a biography of Jesus. We ought to note that Mark has no birth story of Jesus. He starts with the preaching of John the Baptist, and then Jesus comes on the scene, preaching the Kingdom of God.

We have to admire Mark for tackling the task of writing the first Gospel. Remember that this man, John Mark, comes from a family clearly committed to Jesus. The last supper is in the upper room of a home of a man known to Jesus. A young man, possibly this man's son, is among the group in Gethsemane, and is almost arrested, escaping by leaving his clothing—a sheet—in the hands of the soldier attempting to arrest him, and fleeing in his birthday suit. Later we find the 120 followers of Jesus praying in an upper room, perhaps the same as the scene of the last supper. Then we find that when Peter is arrested in the Book of Acts and set free from prison by an angel, he goes directly to the home of John Mark's mother, where the church has gathered to pray for Peter. Later on, Mark's uncle (or cousin; the Greek is unclear) Barnabas arranges for Mark to go on the first missionary journey with Paul and himself.

John Mark leaves his companions in the middle of the first missionary journey and returns to Jerusalem. Guesses are legion as to his reason; what we do have some evidence for is that he became the helper, or secretary, to Simon Peter in his preaching. And then, in Paul's letters we find references to John Mark as a friend and coworker. John Mark is one of the most blessed of men, to have known well and worked with the two greatest followers of Christ in the first century, Paul and Peter. Little wonder that God chose him to write the first Gospel!

So, when the eye-witnesses to the ministry of Christ began to die away, God inspired this young man, John Mark, to write the first Gospel. Not a biography, but an expansion of the preaching of the early Church. Take a look at Peter's Pentecost preaching and you will see that Mark's Gospel emphasis is that of Peter.

Mark's Gospel can be seen as a series of snapshots—Jesus goes here, and there, and does this and that. There are no long speeches as we find in the Fourth Gospel. Jesus is the strong Son of God before whom demons kneel and confess his identity; he calls and men obey; he walks on the water and commands the waves to be muzzled and lie down. He strides through the landscape in the midst of conflict with the religious leaders and goes to the cross. But in him has come the Kingdom of God. And men hear its call—sometimes as a tolling bell, or a screaming siren, or the joyous bells of the wedding. The Kingdom has come, and men can and should enter it now!

You know, this afternoon would be a good time to sit down and read Mark's Gospel, this first Gospel ever, from beginning to end. We will see a portrait of the Strong Son of God, Jesus Christ.

Luke's Portrait of Jesus

Without the Gospel of Luke, how different would be our religious experience! —No manger scenes at Christmas, no parable of the Prodigal Son, no children singing about a little man named Zacchaeus. . . This Gospel rightly been called the most beautiful book ever written; it is my favorite—and perhaps your favorite—-Gospel.

Who is the painter of this beautiful portrait of the Lord? If the painter of Matthew's Gospel is akin to Rubens with his rich colors, with kings dressed in silks and wearing gleaming crowns of gold coming to stand before the child offering kingly gifts; if the painter of Mark's portrait of the Lord reminds us of Michaelangelo's strong, muscular paintings—then perhaps we can think of Luke's style as being like that of Bruegel, the 16th century Flemish painter with his love for the common man—see his *Census at Bethlehem*, in which we cannot even tell who is Mary and Joseph until we notice, in the census line, a woman sitting on a donkey led by a man with carpenter's tools on his back.

Or perhaps Luke is like Rembrandt, with his beautiful painting of an ordinary (and not extremely attractive) dutch mother rocking the cradle while Joseph does carpenter work in the background and angels hover overhead; Rembrandt calls the painting *Holy Family with Angels.* It is interesting that a tradition persists that Luke was actually a painter in oils. The tradition stems from the fifth century, however, and is probably a mix-up of names. He is certainly a brilliant and inspired painter with words.

What do we know of Luke? Well, he was a Gentile; perhaps a former slave of Theophilus. Possibly the brother of Titus, as early church fathers Origin and Chysostom thought, based on 2 Cor 8:18 and 12:8. Some scholars feel he is the man in Paul's vision at Troas. Luke was a companion of Paul—notice the "we" sections of Acts (Acts 16:10-17). Maybe he met Paul on the first missionary journey. Probably he did research on the Gospel and Acts when Paul was in prison in Caesarea. Col 4:14 tells us he is a "fellowworker" of Paul, and a physician.

Notice some of Luke's themes in his portrait of Jesus. *Joy and hope* are central. There are more pure happy scenes, more scenes filled with hope in Luke than in the other gospels. Here is no "man of sorrows", but one who eats and drinks with sinners and pharisees. Luke 15 has as a central theme the **joy** of the kingdom, as the housewife, shepherd and father call in friends to rejoice over their success in finding the lost.

Here is the Man of Prayer. In addition to the instances of prayer found in Mark, Luke has 7 prayers not found in other gospels. Luke tells us about Jesus praying at his baptism, at his transfiguration, and before selecting disciples. Only Luke records Jesus' comment at the Last Supper that he had prayed for Peter. Luke gives us the parables of the Friend at Midnight, the Judge and the Widow, and the Pharisee and the Publican.

Here is the Friend of the Poor. Luke's Nativity is no story of kings coming; but of a child for whom there is no room in the inn. He is born in a stable, and only shepherds come to see him. Only Luke has the story of the Rich man and Lazarus. Notice Luke's version of the beatitudes; Matt says "Blessed are the poor in spirit"—but Luke says simply "Blessed are the poor."

The Emphasis on Women. We know more about Mary from Luke's Gospel than all the others put together. (If we had only John's Gospel, we wouldn't even know her name). Mark refers to her on two occasions, naming her once. Matthew uses her name 5 times in 3 episodes. But Luke mentions her by name 13 times in 5 episodes; and refers to her 3 other times without mentioning her name. Luke's Mary is an example of how God can use a small instrument for great purposes.

This is the Universal Gospel. Simeon, in the temple, proclaims him as a "light to lighten the Gentiles." In his Nazareth sermon Jesus refers to Elijah staying in the home of a Gentile widow in Sidon, and of Elisha healing Naaman.

This is the Gospel of the *sympathizing* Jesus; a portrait of his *compassion*, his feeling-with-others. This is the Gospel of the Seeking Saviour . . .This is the picture of the seeking shepherd, the searching housewife, the waiting father. For me this gospel is summed up in the Christmas Carol, *It Came Upon A Midnight Clear:*

All ye, beneath life's crushing load, whose forms are bending low—
Who toil along the climbing way with painful steps and slow,
Look now! For glad and golden hours Come swiftly on the wing;
Rest beside the weary road, and hear the angels sing.

Perhaps in these trying times we need to rest awhile and hear the angels sing!

John's Portrait of Jesus

Matthew's Gospel is known by the symbol of the lion, Mark's Gospel by a man, Luke's Gospel by an ox, and the Fourth Gospel's symbol is that of an eagle. Do you have an idea why the eagle is John's symbol? Well, as early as perhaps 150 AD, the Christian scholar Clement of Alexandria said, "John, perceiving that the bodily facts had been made plain in the Gospel . . . composed a spiritual Gospel." And so this Gospel is different from the first three.

If you have ever read straight through the Gospels, you have noticed that the first three (Matthew, Mark and Luke, called the synoptic gospels because they basically see the Gospel story alike) begin with either a birth account of Jesus or with the preaching of John the Baptist. But John's Gospel begins with the eternal Word, Jesus, before taking on humanity.

John's Gospel puts Jesus' ministry entirely in the south, around Jerusalem, while the other Gospels have Jesus working completely in the north, in Galilee, until the final journey to Jerusalem. The synoptic Gospels have many parables, while the Fourth Gospel has long speeches and few, if any, parables. John tells us things not in the other Gospels: the wedding at Cana and the raising of Lazarus, for example. John has no demons, as contrasted with Mark especially. The bread and wine at the Last Supper are not mentioned in John's Gospel, but the footwashing is substituted.

Remember that John's Gospel is not written to give new facts, but to meditate on the story you already know. It seems clearly written for those who already know the other Gospels. Oddly enough, while this Gospel was evidently written later than the other three, the oldest manuscript of any of the four Gospels yet found is a fragment of John's Gospel dating from about 130 AD.

It has been customary to hang an outline of John's Gospel on seven major "signs" or events increasingly showing the purpose of Christ's coming into the world. The seventh and most amazing event is the raising of Lazarus, and after that event the Fourth Gospel "goes downhill" to the cross.

John's Gospel strongly connects Jesus with the Old Testament, and perhaps the saddest words in the New Testament are found in John 1:12 where "he came unto his own, and his own received him not." The rejection of Jesus by his countrymen is clear in John, but while many people think John's Gospel is anti-Semitic, there are many positive comments about the Jews of Jesus' time.

The Holy Spirit is emphasized in this Gospel. Four chapters at the close of Jesus' ministry deal with the work of the Holy Spirit. Perhaps it is a simplification, but Jesus' followers felt his presence even after the ascension, and they chose to call this presence the Holy Spirit, the Spirit of Jesus.

This Gospel stresses the relationship of Jesus the Son to God the Father. Over and over the obedience of the Son is mentioned. The Son only does what he sees the Father doing. Whoever has seen the Son has seen the Father. Statements like this fill the Fourth Gospel.

There is another aspect that I find particularly meaningful. At the start of his Gospel John tells us that John the Baptist, talking to two of his disciples, points Jesus out: "Behold the Lamb of God." Then at the close of this Gospel we find that while the other Gospels have Jesus and his disciples eating the Passover before he is crucified, John has that last meal taking place a day before the Passover feast.

In fact, read John 19:28,31,42. What we know is this: on the Day of Preparation, from noon until 3 pm, the priests slaughtered hundreds and perhaps thousands of lambs at the temple mount with ceremonial knives, drained the blood and gave the carcass back to the owner to prepare it for the Passover meal that evening. But over on another mountain, Mt Calvary, another lamb was slain at the same time. And darkness fell from noon until 3 pm as the eternal Lamb of God, who takes away the sin of the world, was slain.

We are not saved by the blood of the lambs slain on Mt Zion, but by that other Lamb, the Son of God. Let us read all four Gospels and rejoice.

One More Time: Luke 5

Sometimes I need to be reminded that the Lord has all knowledge, all power—and a plan for every life! One of my favorite scriptures illustrating those truths is the story of the great catch of fishes in Luke 5. Naturally I turn to stories of great catches of fish in these hot summer days. Last week while flyfishing I saw a whole troop of trout carrying canteens, it's so hot and dry.

Anyway, in the story in Luke we find Simon Peter and his friends have fished all night with no luck. They couldn't beg, borrow, buy or steal a nibble! So, with the coming of the dawn they haul in the nets and head for shore. There they are, cleaning the nets, when Jesus happens by. A crowd is gathering, so Jesus asks Peter for the use of his boat as a pulpit, so to speak.

When Jesus finished teaching—and since the point of the story isn't the content of the teaching, we have no idea what Jesus was saying—he turned to Peter and as payment for using his boat, told Peter to push out into the deep and get ready for a great catch.

Now one reason I like Peter so much is that he is just like you and me. I can see the wheels turning in Peter's mind as he tries to decide whether or not to obey Jesus. He has good reasons to hesitate to do as Jesus commands. First, Peter thinks he knows more about fishing than Jesus. Jesus is no fisherman. Peter has perhaps heard Jesus speak before, and while he is drawn to Jesus, it is clear that Jesus is a carpenter, not a fisherman. Any fisherman on the Sea of Galilee knows that you do not catch fish in the heat of the day. And any nut knows that the fish school near the shore, not out in the deep water.

Through the years I have watched individual Christians, including myself, act as if they knew more than Jesus does about a particular situation. I've seen churches act like that, too! Isn't it odd that we would think we know more about anything in this world than the One who made both us and the world!

The second reason Peter hesitates is that he doesn't want to fail. The shoreline of the Sea of Galilee is dotted with other fishermen, cleaning their nets and perhaps watching this scene. If Peter, against his better judgement, does as Jesus requests and fails, he will be the laughingstock of the fishermen! And more than that, Jesus will look foolish, and will lose face with Peter. Neither of which appeals to Peter. So he hesitates while he thinks things over. He doesn't want to fail.

Now that's normal. Nobody likes to fail. But we all do. And we did. We fell on our face the first time we tried to walk. The first time we swung at a baseball, we hit thin air. But failing is not the real test; the test is whether we get up and try again. I try to remember that as a minister I can make a lot of mistakes; I just try not to make them all in a row.

Well, Peter did what Jesus told him to do, and you know the rest. The nets almost broke with the load of fish. When Peter got back to shore he begged Jesus to go away from him, for he was a sinful man. But you better believe Jesus didn't leave.

Peter did three things that day that he never dreamed of doing when the sun rose: He let a carpenter tell him how to fish, he confessed his sins, and he left his boat and followed Jesus.

You know, something like that could happen to you in church today.

Paralyzed Hands: Mark 6

You are probably familiar with the famous painting of the German artist Durer back in the 1500s, showing praying hands. It is a powerful work and in any religious book store you will find prints of the painting and sculptures of the hands. It makes one think about hands, and I find myself thinking about the hands of God.

Have you ever thought about God's hands?

I remember the child's answer when the teacher told the story of Moses hidden in the cleft of the rock, covered by the hand of God, watching God pass by. *"What do you think Moses was thinking?"* asked the teacher. *"My, what a hand!"* replied the child. When I think about Jesus in the manger, I remind myself that this baby is God. If you had been a child, maybe the son or daughter of one of the shepherds, little hands and feet waving might have been all you would have seen of God Almighty as you stood by the manger that night! Are these little hands the hands of God? Did those tiny fingers fling the stars into space? What are God's hands like? Are they the rough hands of the farmer, or the smooth hands of the person who works indoors? Are God's hands like the pianist's hands or more like the boxer's hands? Maybe it depends on what we see God doing!

When I think of God's hands, I see *creating* hands. In his poem sermon, *Creation*, James Weldon Johnson, the noted black preacher, describes God at the time of the creation as *"throwing a ball of fire into space . . .* and *like a mammy kneeling in the clay* shaping man.

Isaiah the prophet says that God has *"measured out the oceans in the hollow of his hand."* Yet I'm afraid most people think of God's hands in a negative way—the hand of God upon us in *punishment.* Many people see God at work only in his role as Judge. That feeling was put vividly, in colonial times, in the famous sermon of Jonathan Edwards, *Sinners in the Hands of an Angry God.* Brother Edwards described how God dangles us sinners over the fires of hell like puppets on strings, and sometimes he dips us down and the string is singed and we fall into judgment. There is an old Scottish saying of widows, *"The hand of God has touched me."* And the hands of God *are* involved in punishment of sin and in some of the pain and sorrow of our lives. But far more terrible than to fall into the hands of an angry God is to *fall out of the hands of a caring God!*

And when I think of God's hands I think of hands that *rescue and redeem and shape our lives.* That old T-shirt motto that *"God is not finished with me,"* is the Gospel truth! God's hand is still upon each one of us, shaping, moulding us, shutting this door and opening that door, and by his mighty hand bringing his plan for our lives.

And so that story in Mark's Gospel when Jesus preaches in his home synagogue rings so odd. We are told that the people did not believe in him, and therefore he could do no mighty work there! Here is one of the most incredulous statements in the Bible—Jesus unable to do miracles! In that particular case, Jesus was unable to do many miracles because of their *unbelief.*

As damning as their behavior was, it is not as bad as the hands of Jesus being paralyzed by the nonchalance, the complacence, the apathy of his followers! There is an old, worn saying that is worn because it is full of truth: *He has no hands but our hands.* The Gospel must be personalized. The most familiar picture of Jesus is the one of him found in cemeteries, standing with arms outstretched, welcoming all us sinners. But what if those hands are broken and paralyzed through our apathy? When our son Deryl was born at Rex Hospital in Raleigh while I was in seminary, I remember waiting anxiously in the lobby. I also vividly remember, over 40 years later, the life-size statue of Christ in the lobby, standing with hands outstretched—only the hands had been broken, fingers missing here and there.

Go out and offer a helping, loving hand to someone in need. Go offer a sympathic hand to the sorrowing. It's God's hand you're offering.

The Problem with the Bucket: Matthew 6

Funny thing about Matthew's account of the Lord's Prayer. When Jesus finishes teaching this prayer in answer to his disciples' request for him to teach them to pray, he comments on only one phrase in the prayer. Do you remember which phrase it is? He says nothing about the goodness of our Father; nothing about the glories of the Kingdom; not a word about the power of temptation or the need for daily bread. *Jesus only comments on the phrase about forgiveness.* He simply says that if we do not forgive others, God will not forgive us. Is God that much like us? Is God so petty that he will "get you back" if you don't forgive others?

I think Jesus is talking about the bucket effect. Remember those tomato plants you bought last spring? You know, you got a little tray of six of them. After a bit you set them out. And they took off— good soil, plenty of rain, lots of sunshine. Now, what if you had put a bucket over one of them. —I'm not saying you did, but folks do crazy things. If you covered that plant with a bucket for several days, it would die. Just wither up and die. *But the sun is still shining, the soil is still rich, and the rains still fall.* It's the bucket that kills the plant. I think Jesus is saying that if you are unwilling to forgive others, if your heart is full of poison and locked up tight, you put a bucket over your life. And so you are unforgiven. It isn't that God is unwilling to forgive you; it isn't that he plays tit for tat; the truth is that you have shut yourself off from the grace of God!

It's a spiritual law. It's valid for time and for eternity. It's true for yesterday, today and tomorrow. It is true for those who crucified Jesus and it's true for you and your neighbor. *If you won't forgive, you cannot be forgiven.*

Years ago, after I had been at First Church, Memphis for perhaps 10 years, I went to see a lady who had a death in her family. Now in a church that size I couldn't keep up with everybody and know who was in church and who was not. Anyhow, here I was, knocking on her door. She invited me in, and we sat in her living room. I still remember that I sat on the sofa and she in an armchair. We chatted amiably enough for a few minutes as I expressed my sympathy and that of our church in her loss. Then, she suddenly said to me: *"You don't know that I have been mad at you for years, do you?"* To say that I was taken aback is an understatement! I confessed that I wasn't aware of that, and had only noted that she hadn't been in church in some time when we got the news of the death in her family.

She proceeded to tell me how angry she had gotten some 8 or 10 years ago. It seems that the Minister of Education I brought in shortly after I came to the church, a fine young man who went on to teach in one of our seminaries, had made some changes in the Bible Study hour structure, which she attributed to me! When it all began to sink in, I realized that she had been blaming me for nearly 10 years for something I really had nothing to do with. But it was one of those "teachable moments." I explained that I was totally unaware that she was upset about the changes made years back. I went on to say that I was also totally unaware of her anger toward me. I tried to take blame, etc. for what happened years earlier, and got around to pointing out to her that the only one who had been affected by her anger and unforgiveness *was herself.* I hadn't even known about it! She had cut herself off from the fellowship of the church, from its worship and ministry—because she was angry and unforgiving toward me.

Well, the end of the matter was that we prayed about it, talked about putting dead things to rest, and she felt a burden lifted. I was forgiven, and her relationship to the church bloomed once more.

One other thing about those buckets. We put 'em over ourselves; we can take 'em off ourselves. Selah.

The Will of God: Genesis 45; Romans 8

Are you up to a bit of heavy theological thinking this morning? —it is Sunday morning, you know. I don't think there's any religious topic that generates more discussion than *the will of God*. And we twist the Biblical meaning of the will of God for several reasons. One is that this broken evil world does such bad things to us that we cannot cope unless we can somehow think this terrible thing is the will of God. In doing this we often slander God. For instance, a child is killed in a car accident. The cause of the wreck was a drunk driver, who escaped with only scratches. As a pastor I have seen this terrible thing happen in the families of my flock. Over and over the families say, "It was God's will." —Because that's the only way we can handle it. But it wasn't really God's will; it was the stupid, blindless will of a drunk! Yet, of this we can be certain: the will of God is that this child be safe with Him, and that nothing be lost. And even of this event, God will work in it and use it.

Another way we misunderstand God's will is to think it deals primarily with our individual happiness and wealth and our own plans for our life. God's will for each of us begins with our having a relationship of peace and purpose and fulfillment with God through His son Jesus of Nazareth. Our personal selfish plans for happiness are submerged in being a part of His plan to recreate this weary old world through His people, the church.

Yet I believe God does have a will, a plan, for our individual lives. This plan dovetails into the mighty "plan of God for the ages" as Paul put it. And God's plan for your life is filtered down to you through prayer, through your devotional times, through people, through circumstances, in interaction with the devil and the forces of evil. Like the mountain stream which goes laughing and singing and dancing down the mountain, oblivious to the rocks and logs—dancing over and under and around them; the will of God for your life cannot be defeated or turned aside permanently, unless you wish it so. Just consider the life of the patriarch Joseph in Genesis—the longest continuous narrative there. The summary is in chapter 45, where Joseph tells his brothers that God's plan is overarching all our petty strivings.

Perhaps we do not always realize how God uses us to carry out His will in the lives of others. I think one of the best stories I ever heard on the will of God is found in Joe David Brown's grand old novel **Stars In My Crown.** Brown tells how, as a child, he lived with his preacher grandpa. An old black man was a dear friend of the little boy, and one night the white-sheeted men came to lynch old Uncle Famous. You see, while he cared nothing for money, his land sat on rich oil reserves. He wouldn't sell, so they planned to do away with him. Grandpa got word, and came to Uncle Famous' cabin to stay with him that night. The KKK came, and told the preacher to step aside. Grandpa said he'd just come to pray with Uncle Famous and help him prepare to meet his Maker. He said that Uncle Famous was ready to die. It seemed, however, that Grandpa wanted to read Uncle Famous' last will and testament before they took him away.

He took some papers from his pocket and began to read the old black man's will. To one man Uncle Famous left his shotgun—as a boy the man had always wanted to shoot it, although the kick knocked him down; to another he left his fishing rod, because when that man was just a boy he had often fished with Uncle Famous. And the list went on and on, with the white-sheeted men growing more uncomfortable by the minute. Finally they began to shuffle away, much to the old black's surprise. As Grandpa folded the will and pocketed it, a sheet fell to the ground and was picked up by the little boy. "Grandpa—there's no will here—these are blank pages!" Grandpa replied, "Yes, there is, boy, the will of God!" God's will is mediated to other people through your words and actions, and to you through other people!

Busy, Busy, Busy: I Kings 20

I often think of a cartoon in which a frightened young priest—it could just have easily been a Baptist minister!—comes rushing into the office of the bishop in the rear of the cathedral, with a worried look and a wringing of the hands: "Your Reverence, there is a man outside in the congregation who says he is Jesus Christ! What shall I do?" As he came to his feet and began to straighten his desk, the bishop replied, "Look busy, man; look busy!"

This mindset of busyness and work means all too often that our sense of self-worth and the worth of others is tied up with our work, with what we do, rather than who we really are. I remember a tombstone in England on which is carved this epitaph: *Born a man; died a Grocer!* Far more important than what we do for a living is who we are spiritually.

The official hymn of the Protestant work ethic is "Work, For the Night is Coming!" And we generally assume that a man cannot go wrong if he is busy! Most of us find it difficult not to portray ourselves as always busy! So most of us find ourselves in a furious pace of life which we allow to rob us of a deeper spiritual life—or at least we lay the blame on the pace of our lives.

Our problem is well illustrated in an Old Testament story. In 1 Kings 20, Ben Hadad, the king of Aram, goes to war against Ahab, king of Israel, not once but twice. On the second occasion Ahab won the battle by the grace of God. But having won, he let the enemy king, Ben Hadad, go free. Now a prophet of God, hearing about this, had a friend knock him around a bit and, bandaged up, the prophet sat by the roadside until the king came by. Then the prophet cried out to the king, the chariot halted, and the bandaged "soldier" made his plea to the king. It seems that this man, in the heat of the battle, had been given charge of a captured enemy soldier and told to guard him. "If he escapes, either your life is forfeit, or you must pay a ransom!" Well, as the miserable man tells the story in 1 Kings 20:40, "While your servant was busy here and there, he was gone!" The king had no sympathy and declared the punishment just. Then the prophet ripped off his disguise and the king recognized a prophet who then chastised him for letting the enemy go free. Our point is the excuse the man in the story made: *"While I was busy here and there, he was gone."* Yes, that's our problem: *While we are busy here and there, our spiritual life is gone.* While we are busy here and there: making a living, helping at the school, working with the civic club, coaching little league, doing church work, *our spiritual life is being ignored or made a stepchild.*

There is a New Testament example of the same problem in Luke 10. Here we see Jesus as a dinner guest in the house of Martha in Bethany. It is pointed out that Martha owns the home; she is the sensible one with a head for the good old work ethic. In verse 39 we read that she had a sister named Mary, who *also*—mark that word; it is translated *moreover* in some versions—sat at Jesus' feet and listened to his teaching. Now verse 40 says that Martha was *cumbered, distracted* with much serving. Literally, the word pictures one who is actually drawn, pulled around, a twisted expression of seriousness and duty. So poor Martha is taking care of the necessary arrangements and a whole lot of other arrangements that don't matter a bit. But finally she grows irritated at Mary's abdication of duties, and bursts in where Jesus and Mary sit talking, and demands, *"Lord, is it nothing to you that my sister has left me to do the serving? Tell her to carry her end of the load!"* Now notice the reply of Jesus. He tells Martha that she is distracted with many things—many dishes of food for the meal—but really only **one thing** is necessary. And then he adds,

"Mary has chosen the best part, which shall not be taken from her."

There is a message here for us. Consider a couple of truths with me: *(1) Jesus himself practiced and taught that the spiritual world must be our anchor in this material world.* We will all become imitators of the Rich Fool if we ignore that truth.

(2) In this scene Jesus is saying that our relationship to him, the deepening of our spiritual life, is a choice we make. Mary chose that good part. We will not automatically become more spiritual; we must seek it.

But how can we make Mary's choice amid our frenzied pace? First, we must *seriously desire the Kingdom of God first in our lives.* Second, we must develop a plan that provides time alone with God. We have no trouble getting up early to go fishing or hunting or golfing. Perhaps we will need to get up earlier to have a regular devotional time. Third, *we must build upon this devotional time a conscious awareness of the spiritual and eternal dimension of life throughout the week.* Fourth, *we must join our life and our faith with that of others by finding our place in the house of God on the Lord's Day.*

Now let us take stock. Some folks have their priorities backward:

> *They worship their work;*
> *They work at their play;*
> *They play at their worship.*

What about you?

The Lantern of the Lord: I Timothy 1

What do Hank Williams, William Shakespeare, and Herod Antipas all have in common? I'll give you some clues. I thought about singing *"Your Cheatin' Heart,"* for you, but realized you couldn't hear me. Listen to the words of the chorus:

"Your cheatin' heart will make you weep;
You'll cry and cry and try to sleep;
But sleep won't come the whole night through;
Your cheatin' heart will tell on you."

Now a word from Shakespeare's *Richard III* as another clue:

"My conscience hath a thousand tongues,
And every tongue brings in a different tale,
And every tale condemns me for a villain."

Our last clue comes from a scene in Matthew's gospel as Herod Antipas hears of the growing fame of Jesus. *"Who is this Jesus of Nazareth?"* Some said he was a prophet, others said this or that— then Herod broke in with his terse comment: *I know who he is; he is John the Baptist, whom I beheaded, come back from the dead.* One preacher said this is the resurrection not of John the Baptist, but of conscience!

All three men have given us striking examples of the power of the conscience. Conscience compels us to do strange things; there is even a "Conscience Fund" kept by the government to receive money sent in by conscience-stricken folks. It was begun in 1811 when a person sent in $5 for conscience's sake. Now the fund has millions of dollars! There is probably something on your conscience, which means it is doing its work. A bishop once wrote a poem picturing a man sitting down with his conscience and he discovers that

The ghosts of forgotten actions
Came floating before my sight,
And the sins that I thought were dead sins
Were alive with a terrible might.
And I know of the future Judgment,
How dreadful so 'er it be,
That to sit alone with my conscience
Would be judgment enough for me!

A famous comedian quipped that "people would listen to the

voice of conscience if they knew which channel it was on." The conscience doesn't come from Hollywood; it comes from God! Some folks laugh at the whole idea of conscience, and especially the idea of a conscience with super-natural origin. They point to different morals of different cultures and say what we call conscience is but a leftover remnant of tribal memory. The little child knew better than that when he said to his mother one day, "I've got something inside me I can't do what I want to with." And even Huck Finn's got a point when he says that "conscience takes up more room than all the rest of a person's insides."

The conscience is an echo of a will, a law greater than our own desires. Proverbs 20:27 asserts that the conscience is the *candle of the Lord* in the heart of man. Robert Browning called conscience "the great beacon light God sets in us all." And every person on earth is endowed with a conscience. It comes as standard human equipment. Even so, it is true that our consciences can be blunted by our society or by our twisted thinking.

Most of us still have a conscience which can make us miserable— thank God! In one sense the Bible is the record of man's struggle with his conscience; his effort by works and sacrifice to soothe his accusing conscience. All of us want a good conscience and all of us need a pure conscience. Paul speaks of the tragedy of a professing Christian putting away a good conscience and thus making shipwreck of his life (1 Timothy 1:19). All the money in the world, all the one-night stands, all the wild living cannot buy the peace of a clean, pure conscience.We read in Hebrews 9:14 that the only perfect and permanent cleansing and purifying of the conscience requires the blood of Jesus the Son of God. Through his blood the darkest conscience can become as white as snow. To have a conscience that will not mislead either you or others, try this: (1) *seek the constant companionship of Jesus* through his Holy Spirit and prayer above all others; it will enlighten our conscience and give it a steady light on what is right and wrong. (2) *seek fellowship with other Christians* committed to the lordship of Jesus above comfort or culture; it will help to trim the wick of your conscience's candle. And (3) *give serious and careful study to the Scriptures*; they will strengthen your light.

The Man Who Came Back: Psalm 73

In these days we hear a lot about folks leaving the church; about folks changing denominations; and even about how folks who dropped out of church are coming back to church. Somewhere I read that we go to the New Testament to find our salvation; we go to the Old Testament to see how to keep it. These are days filled with war, economic crisis, cynicism and a dozen other stresses that cause folks to lose their relationship with God, so the polls say nothing new.

It is in the Psalms that real people, flesh and blood and hopes and dreams and sins and shame, lay their struggles before us for our edification. And through the centuries, many have found the testimony of a man named Asaph, in Psalm 73, to be the pinnacle of the Psalms, a mirror of our own personal spiritual struggles and victories. This psalm, and the entire book of Psalms, has been a pillar of strength to me and to many through the years.

Consider the man Asaph. "But as for me, I had almost slipped," he says in Psalm 73. He starts at the end of his dark night of the soul. Why had he "almost slipped", stumbled into the pit, fallen off the cliff; almost turned his back upon his faith? How did he get into this fix? What turned him off to church? Was it something the pastor said, or something somebody did? No, he just started looking around at the values of the world, and who seems to be getting ahead. Let him tell it (verses 3-13): he was envious of the arrogant, when he saw how the wicked got rich! He saw how the mean folks didn't seem to get sick and die; they didn't seem to have the troubles most other people have. They are filled with pride; they wear it like a necklace. They ignore and laugh at God; their tongue struts across the earth.

He compared his situation with that of the wicked man. Our man, Asaph, has suffered setbacks; far from being protected by God, he has felt the chastisement of God, and frankly, he began to think: I have kept a pure heart and tried to walk in the right way—and it was all for nothing! After all, most folks then—and now—bought—and buy— into the philosophy of Job's friends who asked him, "Who ever perished, being innocent?" In other words, those who prosper financially and enjoy good health and ignore religion—God must be blessing them! It is an old religion that dies hard.

See the musing of Asaph, the confusion of his heart and mind. Until he decides the value of serving God, he will always be confused and easily discouraged and unhappy in his church relationship. Where did he get help, guidance and peace? In Church; in the house of God (verse 17)! He goes back to church to find the answer to his problem. It is to his credit that he went to church; some go to Las Vegas, some go to bars, some go to the dogs.

He tells us that he realized that he was wrong about the wicked, and also wrong about himself. First, concerning the wicked, he realized that their whole life-style could be swept away in a moment, like a dream. Indeed, he realized that they could be gone like a dream is gone when you awake. And he realized something about himself. He realized that in his proud jealousy, in his envy of the wicked, he had set his heart not on the best life has to offer, but on the second best! That he was jealous of what could be lost in a moment! In church he got his life into focus, and saw that the most important thing in life is our relationship to God. When he realized this, he saw how spiritually immature and foolish he had been.

What happened to him in church? First, he saw eternity looming over time. He saw, above the hustle and bustle and piling up of money and influence in this world—the throne of the eternal God. He was reminded that God's ways are not our ways, and his thoughts are not our thoughts. Second, he saw the Judge of a moral universe. This fellow Asaph had almost forgotten that this is a moral world; that the scales will someday be balanced—if not in this life, then afterwards.

The truth of the matter cannot be better put than the closing words of Asaph: "Lord, whom have I in heaven but you? There is nothing on this earth I want more than you!" He's got his head on straight again! "You will guide me with your counsel, and afterward receive me into glory." No greater need than our need to walk with God, to receive his counsel; no greater hope, no greater reward than to be received into glory, into everlasting heaven, by Jesus.

If you are close to the edge; if this man's story is your story; then this is a good time for you to get your heart and head straightened out—in God's house. Yeah, I know the wicked prosper and the church is filled with hypocrites . . . but it's just the place for folks like you and me.

A Terrible Poison: I Kings 2

You know, I've often pondered that deathbed scene of King David, found in I Kings 2 in the Bible. It's as fresh as today's newspaper. David is dying and the family is called in. I can see him beckoning his son Solomon to come closer and lean over the bed. Then David's dark side comes out. He has kept a log of revenge and now he calls on Solomon to carry it out. "You know how to deal with Joab," he says, "and bring the white head of Shemei to the grave with blood on it." Solomon is a man of action, and carries out a series of bloody deeds of revenge. "So the kingdom was established in the hand of Solomon."

But that seems almost too commonplace to comment upon these days. A few years ago *Reader's Digest* tried to track down the story of the newspaper ad advertising a late model Cadillac for sale for the ridiculous price of $50. Most folks ignored the ad, thinking it to be a joke. One man looked at the car, however, and told the lady who owned it that it was worth tens of thousands of dollars. "Yes, I'm sure I could get that for it," she said, "but I will sell it for $50." The man bought the car and then, with title in hand, asked what was the problem with the car. The lady told him that her husband had recently died and the will stipulated the car was to be sold and the proceeds given to his secretary, who had been so kind to him for many years. Filled with jealousy and revenge, the wife determined the secretary should have as little as possible!

A funeral director once told me about a widow who was apparently so broken up over her husband's death that she could not even make arrangements. Then, at the close of the service, when nobody was around and the casket was being closed, he said the woman took off her wedding ring and pitched it, in anger, some 6 feet into the coffin!

Did you hear about the woman who called about a spool of a certain color of thread from a store, and seeing they had it, asked that they deliver it. The management protested, saying the purchase wasn't worth the cost of delivery. She insisted, reminding them of their slogan that they would deliver. So, an hour or so later, a huge 18-wheeler slowly backed its way into her driveway, blocking the street. Unloading ramps were attached to the rear door of the van. Then, with ceremony, a large refrigerator dolly finally came down the ramp and proceeded up her sidewalk, bearing . . . one spool of thread! Everyone loves to get revenge.

The reasons for revenge are the same today as they were in biblical times. *Custom.* Get your enemies because it's the accepted thing to do; everybody does it. Do unto them before they can do unto you! *Daddy said to.* That was Solomon's justification. How our parents do communicate revenge, prejudice and hatred! And how many hurtful things are done both to individuals and our society under the guise of revenge for wrongs done 150 years ago by people long dead to people long dead.

A third rationale for revenge: *He deserves it!* But think about that. If any of us got what we really deserve in life, we would be most miserable. And a fourth reason given for revenge: *I'll feel better!* Think so? I always feel rotten. Think of the cheap little things you do that come under the heading of revenge—things when you're driving down the road, or things in your marriage. Does it really make you feel better?

Jesus said to turn loose of revenge and lay hold on forgiveness. Yeah, you knew I'd get to what Jesus said sooner or later! Jesus' teaching *destroys evil and redeems the evildoer. Revenge doubles evil and destroys the person.* George Washington Carver, the African-American genius who opened the secrets of the peanut, was once in New York to attend and speak at a conference. He got off the train and hailed a horse-drawn taxi to take him to the hotel. The driver, a white man, refused to drive for a black man. At that, George Washington Carver graciously said that didn't matter; if the driver would get in the cab, Carver would drive! When asked about that incident, Carver said, "I will not allow any man to make me hate him."

Jesus' way—forgiveness instead of revenge—is *an indictment upon the world.* The scorn and ridicule we heap upon the concept of forgiveness instead of revenge shows how far this world is from God's will. And in our literature and on our television screens we glorify revenge. What a commentary!

What does revenge really do? *It hardens hearts, filling them with bitterness.* Revenge *puts me in the center; "I'll get you back!"* But on the Judgement Day, there will be no praise when we say we took revenge because *I was justified. . .*as we have received divine mercy, let us show human mercy. Now go out and shock someone by being nice to them whether they deserve it or not!

. . . Thinking About Hell: Matthew 25

Halloween has become a major holiday, partly due to a renewed emphasis on world religions and occult cults, as well as the endorsement given by the immensely popular Harry Potter books. Rather odd, when you think about it, considering that Halloween really is a Christian holiday. (I know, I know all about the Druid religion origin bit). But the very term Halloween is a corruption of the words "Hallowed Evening." The evening before All Saints Day, when for centuries the church has turned its thoughts to the saints gone on to be with the Lord.

Anyhow, one popular element of Halloween in recent years is the "Judgment House," "Eternity House," or some similar name of a program which is usually sponsored by a church and held in a house. The folks who attend this event are usually shown a drama in which people—youth as well as adults—are killed in accidents, etc.and go to judgment and then either to heaven or hell. Almost all these presentations include a time of commitment to Christ. Critics of these programs rail against the pressure such vivid characterizations place on children's imaginations. As for me, I think I'd rather my child—or in my case these days, my grandchildren—go to heaven scared than to go to hell content! Although I feel our choices are broader than that. And, as a matter of fact, two of my grandchildren did just recently begin to rethink their spiritual lives due to visiting one of these "Judgment House" programs. Selah.

Now, these programs emphasize the reality of hell, which leads me to some observations about hell. Over the decades of my ministry folks would sometimes ask about hell: *Is hell literal? Is it really burning fire? Why is there a hell?* Let's take a few minutes to think about these kinds of questions. The first thing I want to say is that whatever we decide on the many facets of hell, we must put all our thinking in the framework of God's creating man for fellowship, of man's rebellion against God, and of God sending Jesus to die for our sins. Once we get that straight, we can punch a stick at hell!

Some folks think there is no hell—just a heaven. It's humorous to read surveys on heaven and hell and see that a much larger percentage of Americans believe in heaven than believe in hell. That's wishful thinking. Some folks believe hell is simply purgatory—that all of us go there to be "purged" of our sins. Some stay there a lot longer than others! This view, too, is wishful thinking in my judgment. A third view is that there is neither heaven nor hell; this life is all there is. No so.

The Bible indicates that hell, like heaven, is a place. Jesus tells us, in Matthew 25, that hell was prepared for the devil and his angels. So if you go to hell, you'll barge into a place not prepared for you, but for the devil. Hell, according to the Bible, is a place of punishment. It may be burning fire. Now don't let my next sentences turn you off. In the broad scheme of things I am considered a conservative Christian. But if you insist on a literal fire in hell, I remind you that Jesus referred to hell as the "outer darkness," the city dump of Jerusalem—Gehenna, weeping and wailing and gnashing of teeth, as well as burning fire. Here's my take on the literal fire. It may be just that. But then again, it is clear to me that the fire may be a symbol of something worse. And just remember that the symbol is never as powerful—or as dreadful—as the reality it pictures.

Perhaps the question of the purpose of hell ought to be considered. I don't think God delights in seeing people frying in hell. Islam's *Koran* says that sinners in hell are roasted until their skin begins to crackle, and then they are shucked out of that hide and given a new one to keep on burning! (Surah 4:56). More to the point, it seems to me that the New Testament teaches that hell is the trash can of eternity. Gehenna was the valley just southwest of the walls of Jerusalem, a vast trash heap of garbage thrown over the walls. It is one of the chief images of Jesus concerning hell. If we have not found fellowship with God to our liking here and now, will we be happy in His presence in the next world? There really is no answer but the trash can for those who reject God.

Worst of all, hell is the lack of fellowship of God. The meanest man in this county knows that he can call a minister any time of day or night and he will come to bring help and spiritual hope. But to be in hell is to be out of God's mind, out of God's heart; out of God's memory; to have no hope or help, nobody to call in the night.

Well, contrary to the above, I really have no interest in the temperature or furniture of hell. I don't plan to go there. And God has done all He can in Jesus to keep us all out of hell. Take your Bible, go sit out under a beautiful tree and read of the love of God. There's far more of that in the Bible than there is of hell. And, see you in church Sunday.

How To Use Perfume: Mark 14

Have you ever really cruised the perfume aisle of a store and noticed the titles of the perfume? Men, it's an eyeopener! These women really do plan to ambush us! In fact, that's the name of one perfume. Some of the others that ought to give us pause include *Spellbound, All About Eve* [we know about Eve; she was the one with the apple, or was it a pear. . .], *Just Me, Diamonds and Rubies, Prelude* [to what?] and then there's *Poison* [a giveaway if ever I saw one!] and the old standby perfumes: *Charlie* and *Channel No. 5.*

A stroll down the perfume aisle turns a preacher's thoughts to a story in the Bible about perfume, and how a woman used it. The story is found in Matthew 26, Mark 14, and John 12. There is a variant account, some folks think, in Luke 7. The background is the last week in Jesus' ministry. The tension between Jesus and the religious authorities is strung ever tighter; the anger of the devil is boiling over; the plots against Jesus are bubbling. During the days of this last week he goes into Jerusalem to teach, and at evening comes back to the peace and quiet of the little village of Bethany. We are told that some of his friends want to give a feast in his honor—*just to say we love you.* The three accounts have some differing detail, and it is possible that it is held in the house of Simon, a cured leper, who may have been Martha's husband. And Lazarus is one of the guests. Mary comes into the story late as, in the midst of the feast, she comes into the area of the men's feast and pours a bottle of expensive perfume on Jesus.

When she does this, the scene freezes—the perfume permeates the whole house; there is a shocked silence, broken only by Mary's weeping. Tears of gratitude for the raising of Lazarus, perhaps also for the healing of Simon, perhaps also for her own recovery from a hopeless life if she is to be identified with the woman in Luke 7. But the silence is quickly broken by a snort and grumble from a disciple: *"This perfume is wasted! It could have been sold for 300 denarii* [300 days pay for an average worker] *and used to feed the poor!"* Indeed, she poured about 12 ounces [a Roman pound] of pure spikenard, an expensive perfume, on Jesus. John says it was Judas who criticized Mary, and not because he was thinking of the poor, but because he was a thief!

Regardless of the source and motivation of the criticism, Jesus speaks up for Mary. He says she has anointed his body ahead of time for burial. He goes on to say the poor will always be with us, with opportunity to help them when we will, but he will not always be with the disciples and the folks there that day.

May I point out three great truths in this little story about how a woman "wasted" the perfume? First, this story tells us that *there are times when the common-sense view of life fails.* Sure, she could have given the money to the poor—but love and gratitude demanded she do something beyond common sense for Jesus. It wasn't common sense to build the ark when it wasn't raining, but Noah did. It wasn't common sense to confront Goliath with only five stones and a sling-shot, but David did it. It isn't common sense to stand before a church and say that God has called you to be a missionary or minister, but

it's done every Sunday.

Second, this story tells us that *some things have to be done when the opportunity presents itself or be lost forever.* Jesus says Mary read the signs of the times better than the disciples! She felt the end of his ministry was at hand. She, perhaps unconsciously, was preparing him for burial. Often, when we can only say, "I wish I had . . ." we have just passed up one of those "do-it-now opportunities."

And third, this story says that *the fragrance of a lovely deed lingers on down through the years."* Jesus said that whereever the Gospel should be preached throughout the world, this story of what she did would be told. Men may not have good memories for lovely deeds, but God does. And in the Judgement Day every good deed shall be revealed.

What are you doing with the perfume of your life? Pouring it at the feet of an idol, or at the feet of Christ?

Chapter Five

Modern Parables

The Parable of Happy Valley

A few weeks ago, we had some visitors from the flatland country over in West Tennessee. As we stood on the deck at *Rocky Comfort* and contemplated the beauty of the vista before us, I pointed out the Green Mountain, Winding Staircase, Haunted Cove and some of the other fascinating landmarks between the Parkway and Lenoir. Later we went for a drive down Sampson Road to Happy Valley. As we drove along and talked, I realized that this delightful area is more than geography; it is a parable of life.

Most of us rush, rush, rush through our lives. We work like slaves in order to pretend we are living like kings. But we could learn something from slowing down, and visiting a place like the old country store in "downtown Buffalo Cove." You can even get credit there, you know, if you are over 100 years old and have your parents with you! There's something that calls out to my soul when I look at the old antiques and the calendar from Ike's presidency and the old post-office there in the store. We bought hamburgers and some old-fashioned soft drinks and went down the road a bit to the peaceful little park to have a picnic. Not many communities have a beautiful stream flowing by the picnic ground, a lovely playground with toys, and no fence, no sign saying *Keep Out.* But then, this is the Happy Valley. Thank you, Buffalo Cove Baptist Church, for keeping up the park.

Moseying along, we showed our friends Fort Defiance, the colonial fort and then later, the name of General William Lenoir's home in Happy Valley. Have you read the little booklet, *Hand in Hand*

Through the Happy Valley—obviously it is a period writing, but it reaches out to something in us that gets overlooked in the rush and secularism in which we live. It's the story of two little girls in the Lenoir family who died as children in 1877. Don't miss the special days in the fall and at Christmas time at Fort Defiance, as volunteers dress in period costumes and give tours through the house.

And then we showed our friends the Patterson School, and the beautiful little church, the *Chapel of Rest.* Several years ago, when we first saw that magic place, my daughter said she wanted to get married in that little chapel, and sure enough, last summer she did. It's a perfect place for a quiet time of meditation and thoughtfulness about who we are, why we are here, and what life is all about.

We pointed out to our friends Indian Grave road, and the area at the top of the mountain where the mound could be seen in years past. And we reflected on the folks who lived in this valley before the white man came. Was it also their happy valley? Just down the road a bit is a little white church with the charming name, *Just a Closer Walk Baptist Church.* If we were honest about our spiritual condition, the place would be packed every Sunday! By the time we reached Highway 321, the parable had ripened to full form.

Life is like that. We want to be always on the mountaintop in our spiritual lives, but nobody gets out of this world without going through the valley. With our faith to help us interpret life, it can be a happy valley, regardless of the shadows. And there are some graves in every valley, no matter how quaint or beautiful. But, just a closer walk is what we all need. John Bunyan, the author of *Pilgrim's Progress,* would waste no time in telling us that while passing through even the happy valley, we must be an outpost of heaven, a fort of defiance against the devil and his wiles.

I guess Bill the painter first introduced me to Happy Valley when I asked him where he lived. When we bought *Rocky Comfort* and began to do extensive remodeling, it seemed that Bill was a member of the family—he was at our house, painting, all the time! Bill, you do have a happy valley! May God grant us all a closer walk with our Lord through the mountains and valleys of our lives.

Anybody There?

"It was a dark and stormy night . . ." as Snoopy always said when he started out to write a novel while pecking away at his battered typewriter atop his doghouse. That, by the way, has been described as the worst beginning a novel could have. But, as a matter of fact, it was a dark and stormy night. It happpened a week or so ago up in the hills. It was a real storm. High winds, the lightning dancing in the distance and lighting up the room in flash-bulb style. And the rain— it came in sheets, pounding so hard at the windows that I thought it was hailstones at times. Ray the weatherman had warned us. But it was a duzy! In the midst of all this, about three in the morning—two fifty-five a.m. to be exact—our front doorbell rang. It was so weird that it took a moment for the fact that it was the doorbell to register!

I couldn't imagine who—or what—might be at our door at three in the morning in the midst of a driving storm. Adrinline pumping, I leaped out of bed and ran into the closet for clothes. The only reasons I could think of for a visitor at the door at this ungodly hour in this storm were terrifying: a neighbor had dropped dead (or died in his sleep) and a distraught widow was standing there in the storm at my door; someone had crashed into a tree on the way home and had limped up to our door (even though nobody comes by our house on the way home) and other dark scenarios filled my mind. I dashed for the front door, yanked it open, took a faceful of wind and rain, and stared into the dark. *Nobody there.* Nobody there? How can this be? After I retrieved my wits, I began punching the doorbell. It kept on ringing. I shut the door and stared at the box high on the wall, donging away merrily. Several minutes later, just when I had decided to go downstairs and pull the electrical breaker, the doorbell stopped ringing on its own.

I suppose it was a close lightning strike that started it ringing. But whatever reason, it ruined my night. I lay in bed thinking about it for a long time. For some reason, the incident seemed so weird, so strange. I guess it was the lightning, the driving rain, the jumping to the conclusion that some poor soul was in deep trouble and standing at my door.

Anyhow, it set the old sermon machine running for the rest of the night. You know, in the book of Revelation we have the picture of Jesus standing outside the door, knocking for entrance. And there are a lot of folks who will suddenly find him at their door in the midst of a storm, or in the middle of the night. For some folks it will be a heart attack or a car wreck that brings them face to face in a moment of storm with Jesus. For others, it will be some non-fatal good or bad crisis in life—an illness, the birth of a child, the death of a friend or family member, that will thrust them into a meeting with Jesus. And that meeting may lead to a wonderful relationship both in this world and the next. You know, most folks who come to hear the Gospel as adults come through a crisis of some sort, whether good or bad.

I suppose the word to carry away is this: don't wait for a storm to make you aware of your mortality; to make you aware of the truth of the Gospel; to bring you face to face with Jesus. And, don't wait for a storm to bring a neighbor to your door—be a friend, a helper of others, even when the sun is shining.

I Heard a Whistle Blowing

Someone asked me the other day if I were serving as an interim pastor somewhere or if I finally retired . . . Have you ever heard of a minister retiring? Nope, that doesn't happen. I am, however, enjoying a few months of visiting various churches and preaching here and there until the next interim pastorate comes knocking at my door. Right now I have been preaching for a quaint little church near my home between Blowing Rock and Boone.

I say it is a quaint little church because it is a mite unusual in a couple of ways. This church has Henry the Banjo player, for one thing. Henry plays along on the hymns, and during the offertory he and the pianist do some marvelous renditions of hymns. I told the church that Henry is a real treasure. Perhaps you've seen a banjo player helping with the hymns . . . I haven't.

The other thing that makes this church different is that it is Tweetsie's church. That's right. A lot of folks who visit Tweetsie—perhaps even your family—think that the little cemetery right in the heart of Tweetsie is a fake cemetery, just to carrry out the idea of the western "Boot Hill." Not so; that cemetery is the cemetery of Middle Fork Baptist Church, where Henry plays the banjo. And I bet a lot of folks who ride the train at Tweetsie notice that at one point they look down on a quaint little church; they probably wonder where that church is located. I'll tell you.

The other Sunday—I did tell you that I have been preaching for that little church for the past few Sundays, didn't I?—the other Sunday, just as I got up to begin the sermon, Tweetsie's whistle sounded off, coming 'round the bend above the church. Yes, the church you see as you ride Tweetsie is Middle Fork Baptist Church, Tweetsie's church.

Some folks don't like to hear the whistle in the middle of a sermon. I rather like the idea; after all, the church and the world were never meant to pass like ships in the night—or travel on parallel tracks going in opposite directions, if you prefer. I had a seminary professor who used to say ministers ought to preach with the Bible in one hand and the daily newspaper in the other hand! What he meant was that the Bible has something to say to the headlines. The Bible is as relevant as the headline news on TV.

So, let the whistle blow. It reminds us that while we preach the Bible and gather at the church building because it is God's Word and we are God's People—we must interface with the world around us. A world seeking entertainment, fun, escape and nostalgia. The word

I have for Middle Fork church and your church is to never forget that we are commissioned to take the Gospel to a needy world; don't run from it; rather seek ways to interface with our society. The world that is always in decay and sin ought to be brought, every Sunday, face to face with the world that is eternal.

Well, the next time you decide to go to Tweetsie on a Sunday, come early and drop by Tweetsie's church, Middle Fork church, for worship before you visit the cemetery in Tweetsie and ride the train. And don't forget to look for Tweetsie's church when you come 'round the bend—either on the train or on US 321. Because Middle Fork, Tweetsie's church, is just beyond Tweetsie, a couple hundred yards up Bishop's Ridge Road.

Did I hear a whistle blow?

God, We've Got a Problem!

Have I told you the funny story about the little boy and his eye-ball? No? Good, because it's one of my favorite stories. You remember Jesus said a little child shall lead us! It happened a handful of years of ago, on an afternoon when I had gone to my optometrist to see about getting new glasses. He had examined my eyes and had me waiting in a chair in a back hallway while he took care of a little boy who I shall call Johnny. I'm sitting there doing whatever busy ministers do when they simply have to sit and wait, when the doctor comes striding by with a little fellow, perhaps five years old, in tow. As they pass me, the doctor is saying something like, "Now we're going to go down here and look at the back of your eye." Little Johnny took on the oddest expression when he heard those words, and I heard him say in a plaintive voice as he passed me, "Doctor, I think we've got a problem; I don't know how to turn my eye around yet!" The doctor, who was a member of my church, and I have had many a chuckle over that incident.

But you know, I feel a little like that boy when I pick up the newspaper or turn on the TV news. Everywhere we look, greed and graft,
hate and envy, war and strife seem to have the upper hand. From the
oil companies bloated with profit to the growing threat of a world-
wide war between Islam and the west, it seems that things are out of
hand with no answers in sight.

I feel like hollering out to God, "God, we've got a problem; we
don't know how to live in peace with all mankind, and we don't
know how to beat back our greed and care for one another, and we
don't know how to respect one another even if we do not agree on
religion. God, things look mighty bad down the road. We don't know
how to avoid a nuclear war; we don't know how to wean ourselves
from our oil habit; we don't know who's going to feed the starving
millions tonight."

I know how that little fellow felt about his eyeball! But the reason
we can laugh about his situation is because we have a larger perspective, more knowledge, more confidence in the doctor than he had!
And perhaps that's what we need as we survey the mess our world is
in these days. We need a larger perspective; the understanding that
God is in charge of this world. Oh, we can't blame the mess we're in
on God, I don't mean that. We—with the Devil's help—created this
twisted world of man and nature in which we live. But, *it is still God's
world*, and He will have the last word. God expects us to do our very
best to right wrongs and be good stewards of our creation, but the
final outcome is in God's hands.

I hope that the world leaders who are truly Christian find strength
and guidance in prayer, in God's Word and in the realization that God
is ultimately in control. I also hope that each of us, in the confusion
and brokenness of our own lives, can take strength in the realization
that God's will is surely and ultimately going to be done in our little
personal worlds.

So, take hope, Johnny! We're not counting on you to turn your
eyeball around. In fact, most of us adults still can't do that!

The Magical Spring of Huckleberry Knob

A week or so ago we had our annual meeting of property own-
ers of Huckleberry Knob—where all the women are beautiful and
the children are strong—and I gave my annual report on the water
system. You see, the first 15 or so families to discover this enchanted
mountain piped their water from the spring. Somehow, the oversight
of this water system has fallen to me.

This year I included in my report—with tongue in cheek and a
smile— the progress toward bottling this miraculous spring water
and making us all millionaires. I had a half dozen or so samples of
the bottled water, and I read the label, which features the picture of
a beautiful young lady (you can't sell anything without having a fair
lady featured) in the center with the following text: *Mountain Mist
Natural Blue Ridge Spring Water from the Famous Springs of Huckleberry Knob.* On one side of the label is a picture of Atwater Heep,
the Indian, and the story of Huckleberry Knob's famous natural Blue
Ridge Mist springs as follows:

"In the distant past, the Cherokees, a proud Indian tribe, roamed
and fished and hunted the area of Huckleberry Knob. For centuries
the springs on the Knob were known for their healthful, lifegiving,
aphrodisiacal qualities. The last Indian in this area, known by the
white man—for a phrase he kept saying—as "That watta heapum
good," or "Atwater Heep," lived in a stone hut only a few yards
from the springs. In his old age, he kept records of the cures of the
spring water, and passed them on to his "white man" friends. Now
the amazing qualities of the springs of Huckleberry Knob can enrich
your life, too."On the other side panel is found information about the
spring water, including its amazing restorative powers (expressed as
percentages of cures) as gleaned from the records Atwater Heep kept
in his later years: Aphrodisiac 100%; Cures— Warts 50%; Snakebite

100%; Lovesickness 85%; Poor Eyesight 30%; Leg Weakness 65%; Backaches 95%.

After reading the label, I made some comments about our plans to have the entire world drinking our magical spring water within a decade. I pointed out that we have an extensive TV and radio ad campaign ready to go in the near future. As part of that, we have some unsolicited endorsements of our Blue Ridge Mountain Mist spring water from residents on the Knob. (They are so unsolicited that the folks who said these things don't even know they said them!) I'll share a couple with you:

Here's what Mr. Bernie Westinghouse, a native of Germany who owns multiple homes in various resort areas says: "For years I have had a cottage near the springs, but as I grow older I realize the remarkable qualities of Blue Ridge Mountain Mist spring water, and I am just completing a large addition to my home on the Knob so I can have this elixir all the time." (He said a lot more, but some of it was in German).

Here's what Mr. Ted Iceman, who is a seasonal visitor from Florida, says: "For many years I have enjoyed Blue Ridge Mountain Mist spring water, not really realizing how remarkable its powers are. But since I have been playing the violin, I find that this water gives me a nimbleness that I never had before; my fingers are the envy of the entire orchestra in Florida!"

And, too numerous to mention are the accolades for Blue Ridge Mountain Mist spring water from folks in the area who have pets. Some folks report their chihuahuas fearlessly taking on bears since drinking the spring water, and others have been obliged to take their pets to the vet due to the amorous effect of the water.

We know that you will be watching for further news of Blue Ridge Mountain Mist on the CNN network television and local radio, and we will try to keep you informed at this end. And, by the way, the National Park Service has designated the springs a national treasure and have urged us to let them put a Parkway exit just above the

springs for visitors. The water board is pondering the environmental impact of such a move.

Well, I expect that next summer, my annual report might reflect either the unexpected failure of our venture . . . or its amazing success! If you're interested in signing up now for the bottled water . . .

I had fun playing with the spring water idea, but it set me thinking that folks have been looking for a fountain of youth, a magic rejuvenating elixir, for centuries. And the only truly life-changing water I know about is the water Jesus promised the Woman at the Well in John 4. Check it out, and talk with your pastor. And I'll see you around the Knob.

In Praise of "P'Like"

Do you remember "P'Like" as a child? We used to play it all the time—you know, "P'like I'm the cowboy and you're the Indian" or "P'like we're in the army." That was during the Second World War, and since I was the youngest of our gang, I had to "p'like" I was Tojo or some bad guy!

But there's tremendous value in "P'like." In fact, every church I know would be blessed if they used their imagination a lot more. It's a Biblical concept, this idea of imagining that which is not yet; and of using the imagination to see what could be. Jesus urged the disciples to see—in John 4—not people coming through the wheat fields in their white robes; but the ripened stalks of wheat. The harvest was already here, not four months away. In the eleventh chapter of the book of Hebrews we read of Abraham, Isaac and Jacob who looked into the distance and saw a heavenly city, not built by hand. And although they never set foot in this city built by God, they imagined it and it was so in their hearts and minds. Of Moses it is said in the same chapter that he endured, as seeing Him who is invisible. And then there is Elisha's servant, who rose one morning and glanced out the door to see the Syrian army encamped along the hills surrounding the house. When he reported this to Elisha, this prophet sent the servant to look again, and this time he saw the invisible—the chariots of the army of God.

"Where there is no vision, the people perish." And it is so. At Pentecost Peter quoted from the prophet Joel who quotes God, that "your old men shall dream dreams, and your young men shall see visions." In defending himself Paul declares he was not disobedient to the heavenly vision which he saw. Did anyone else see what Paul saw? The prophet Isaiah has the experience of God's call when, in the year that King Uzziah died, he saw in the temple the Lord himself, high and lifted up. The garments of the Almighty swept over the sanctuary, and smoke filled all the room. Do you suppose everybody in the temple that day saw what Isaiah saw?

The people most fruitfully used of God are those folks who could see the invisible, who could use their "sanctified imagination" to see what many could not see, or did not want to see. I am sure that 90% of the churches represented by folks who read this column have been stronger, more vital churches in the past than they are today. Perhaps the high water mark in your church was 30 or 40 years ago. One of the keys to revitalizing our churches is to imagine what God would do and could do with our church. Try an experiment with me. *Can you see in your mind your church filled with folks worshiping God? Can you see the pews filled with boys and girls, mothers and fathers?* Notice that I am not asking you to *remember when* the church was full, back there years ago. I'm asking whether you can see it full *now*.

If you cannot see it; you cannot do it. As King David led a pledging of resources to build the temple, he prayed in I Chronicles 29 that God would keep "the imagination of the thoughts of the temple in the hearts of the people." There is tremendous spiritual power in the ability to see the unseen. It gives the power to do the undoable. Why not have a congregational "town hall meeting" in your church, and let

people share what they can see happening in your church through a sanctified imagination. Remember, if you can see it in your heart and mind, you can do it! Let's be children again: let's "P'like" our way to spiritual health and a greater vision and usefulness to God.

Musings on Stained Glass Windows

Being a retired pastor and doing interim pastorates does have its advantages! I have time to do more extensive Bible study and prepare powerpoint presentations on various studies which I share with churches, such as a study on the Parables of Jesus, a study on How We Got Our Bible, a study on the Book of Revelation, a study on The Hymns We Sing, a study on Spiritual Gifts, and on and on.

I illustrate these studies with paintings of the Old Masters, and with some of the beautiful stained glass windows from the great cathedrals, many of which we've visited. So, this morning I spent a couple hours searching for photos of stained glass windows illustrating Matthew's Portrait of Christ, part of a series I'm doing at my present church.

During a break to have a bit of lunch, I fell to musing about why the great cathedrals—and many of our churches today—have marvelous stained glass windows. The answer is simple, and for the same reason that cathedrals soar upward. When you walk into one of the great cathedrals, your eyes are naturally drawn upward, upward, to the vast stone vault far above. One cannot help but be aware of our smallness and the greatness of God. It is, indeed, concrete teaching of a great truth!

Back in the Middle Ages, in the time of the building of the great churches, most folks were poor people of the soil. Life was hard. And it was a tremendous comfort to go to church and lift up your head and heart and feel that, above and beyond your own smallness, there was a loving God who is in control. Above the turmoil and griefs and struggles of this life, there was God. *Sursum Corda! Lift up your heart!*

And then when your gaze left the vault, there were the huge stained glass windows. Windows filled with images from the Bible; scenes like Noah and the Ark, Daniel and the Lions, David and his harp. And the stories of the Gospel, the parables, and especially the pivotal events in the life of Jesus.

Why was this? Simple: to tell the Gospel story; to help people become familiar with the stories of the Bible and the life of Jesus. Most of the common folks couldn't read, which wasn't a hindrance in their worship, since there were no individual Bibles anyway! Only the clergy, the monasteries and the convents, the rulers and the powerful, could read and afford a handwritten manuscript of the New Testament. Remember that printing—the moveable type press—wasn't invented until in the early 1500s.

As I pondered the beautiful windows which told the Gospel story for unlearned folks, I found myself thinking we need to do more to present the Gospel story in ways other than just reading it. Not that our congregations cannot read; perhaps it is that the ability to read has made the story less precious, even! I reflected on the fact that in the last few Sundays, I have taken the offering plates after the collection of the tithes and offerings, and held them high for all to see that we were offering this money, these tithes and offerings, to God. My statement and prayer as I held the plates high was to ask God to make this a worthy offering, and us worthy people of His grace. Interesting that the offering has increased since I started reminding folks in a vivid way what we are doing!

We preachers are perhaps too fixed on the spoken word, and miss great opportunities to present the Gospel in other ways. I've begun to reflect on ways we can act out, as living stained glass windows, the Gospel that we say has transformed us. Of course, the ordinances do this in a marvelous way.

I remember the definition of a stained glass window given by a little girl in the congregation when asked to explain the figures of the disciples and other saints in the windows. Her reply: "Saints are people the light shines through." I couldn't say it any better. I hope my actions, my life, is truly a stained glass window, and that the light shines through me!

Sursum Corda! Lift up your heart, and let Jesus shine through you.

Have You Lost Anything in Church Lately?

Did I ever tell you about Zona? No? Well, Zona was a most unusual person. When I first met her, she was in her eighties. She had gone through the troubles and tragedies of life common to most of us, from the loss of a husband to problems with children, grandchildren, etc. She passed away a handful of years ago, over 100 years old. Imagine touching three centuries with your life! She did—her gravestone reads: born 1899, died 2002.

But I stray from what I wanted to tell you about Zona. She was a most faithful member of my congregation. If the church doors were open, she was there. Cheerful, always possessing a good word. As she got older—in her nineties—I would recognize her on the Sunday closest to her birthday, ask her to stand so the congregation could see her, both those in the sanctuary and those who were worshipping with us by television. Well, she gradually began to respond to my birthday congratulations with longer and longer speeches, standing there in her pew. I suppose some folks felt it was a bit inappropriate, the service being televised and all. But I felt that anyone who was creeping up on a century of life had earned the privilege of speaking her mind!

But again I stray. During one of those years in her nineties, something happened to her in church that always brings a smile when I remember Zona. One of her great-granddaughters, a preschooler, was attending church regularly with her mother. And sometimes the child would sit with her great-grandmother, and sometimes she would sit way in the back of the sanctuary with her mother. Well, on this particular Sunday she was sitting with Zona about three or four pews from the front. I had just finished the children's sermon and had sent the children back to their pews.

Now Zona wasn't a deep theologian; she trusted her pastor to be theologically correct. She had so much trust that quite often she went to sleep during the service and left the driving to me! On this Sunday, she dozed off during the Children's sermon, and when her great-granddaughter started back to her seat with Zona, seeing that Great-grandmother was asleep, the child decided just to keep on going and sit in the back of the church with her mother. So far, so good.

Zona almost broke up my sermon a few minutes later. She finished her nap in the middle of my sermon, and remembered that her great-granddaughter was sitting with her. But Zona looked around, and no child was on the pew with her. A perplexed expression took charge of her face, and Zona began a search. She looked at the pew in front of her, and the pew back of her. No child. She was sitting on the end of the pew, so she peered out into the aisle, looking down to the front toward me and back up the aisle to the main entrance doors. No child. She managed to get down and look under her pew, but still no child. For the rest of the service she wore a puzzled expression, looking up and down the aisle every now and then. All around her, smiles were evident, and I had a hard time keeping my mind on the sermon! Zona was convinced she had somehow lost a child right there in the churchhouse in the middle of the service!

Well, if you doze during the service, you may lose more than the train of thought of the preacher! Clearly, however, there are some things you ought to lose in church. True worship leads us to lose thoughts of anger, revenge, jealousy toward other people. True worship has a way of flowing through our minds and hearts and having a cleansing effect. We find that we lose our guilt and find forgiveness;

we lose our complacency and find deeper commitment.

Why not lose something at church next Sunday!

Watch Those New Cameras!

I bought a new digital camera recently. That was the first mistake of this tale. Then, a couple weeks ago I got the bright idea of painting a self-portrait—I mean, Rembrandt and all the great painters did that, right? What's that; Rembrandt's self-portraits all seem to have either a wild look in his younger ones or a worried look as he grew older? Never mind. Well, setting out to do a self-portrait was my second mistake. I've done landscape painting for years and have found a large measure of satisfaction and a small measure of financial success in that genre. But portrait painting is a horse of another color, so to speak. Yet, in these days between interim pastorates, it sounded like a good thing to do.

I thought it appropriate to take a few photos of myself to use for reference in the painting, rather than have to look back and forth at a mirror for this painting. Well, I discovered I had purchased a camera far too honest for comfort. It is a Nikon camera with 12 megapixels, for those of you who are into such matters. I held the camera out, pointed it at myself and struck a few of those poses you associate with Napoleon or such folks. After snapping a half dozen or so photos, I downloaded them to my computer.

There's a little bit of poetry which makes a pun on our looks, saying that we know our faces aren't a prize, but we stand behind it, and the folks out front get the shock. Well, as I brought up that photo on my computer I certainly got the shock! It captured in all the detail my flawed features, including the beard stubble and every wrinkle! Oddly, all I could think of as I surveyed my facial wreck was the teaching that the Bible is like a mirror, revealing all our faults and failures!

And so I reflected again that the Bible is alive, probing our hearts and lives. It reveals our deepest sins, our hidden lusts, our hopes and dreams. Thankfully, the Bible does not shout these shortcomings from the rooftop, but acts as a Judge within our hearts, leading us to evaluate and hopefully come to repentance. The Bible is indeed a judge, a ruler, a guide, a mirror of the inner workings of every person's heart. Maybe that's why it's not read much in our times.

Jesus' parables in the Bible are matchless stories. If you haven't read a bunch of them lately, I urge you to do so. And remember that they are not just stories, but mirrors of how certain folks reacted to the Gospel back then, and how we react to the power of the Gospel in our lives today. You'll no doubt see yourself in some of the characters there.

Well, I've painted my self-portrait. Seems I caught most of the flaws the camera pointed out, and then some. But it's really not a bad portrait, and as I told my wife, when I find the fellow I've painted, I think I'll give him this portrait!

And, don't worry, I'm not going to cut off my ear as one of the most famous painters did. You know, as I think about it, he too was a minister early in his career! I guess I had better go look in the mirror and keep on painting.

Procrastination

You should have been in the service last Sunday at Center Grove, the little country church I'm serving as interim pastor. During the children's time with the pastor, we talked about procrastination. I had the kids repeat the word several times before they got the pronunciation and the meaning together! But they already knew about the problem of "putting off doing what you ought to do." I asked for examples in their own lives, and you should have seen the hands go up! . . .Not picking up clothes, not doing homework, etc. etc . . . the

list was impressive. But the problem of procrastination—"never do today what you can put off until tomorrow"—is not confined to children. It is a problem that affects all of us. What husband isn't guilty of procrastination on his "honey-do" chores? Through procrastination the student may lose a scholarship; the salesman may lose the biggest sale of his career; the investor may lose a fortune; the general may lose the battle.

But as I told the folks last Sunday, spiritual procrastination is even more devastating. With spiritual procrastination, you put your immortal soul in danger. The Bible is pretty tough on this business of spiritual "putting off." Remember the man who told Jesus he would like to follow him, but "let me go bury my father first." The man didn't mean his father lay a corpse in the funeral home that day—rather, he wanted to wait until his aged father died before following Jesus. And Jesus' answer shows what he thought of that: "Let the dead bury the dead—you come and follow me." Let the spiritually dead bury the physically dead—you come on now!

And then there's that funny little parable about people procrastinating about entering the Kingdom of God. In Luke 14 Jesus tells a story about a grand supper. The preliminary invitations had been delivered, and now the servant is making the rounds to announce that tonight the banquet will be held. One man gets a pained look on his face and tells the servant to have him excused—he has just bought a field and needs to go see it. A second man allows that he has just purchased 5 yoke (pair) of oxen and must go check them out; please have him excused. And the third man has just married a wife, and of course cannot attend the banquet. Now Jesus picked these excuses; it shows what God thinks of our spiritual procrastination! Whoever heard of buying land and *then* going to look at it! And how ridiculous to think a man had purchased 10 oxen without checking them out first. Sure, "don't look a gift horse in the mouth," but these oxen are not gifts—the man is paying good money and claims he hasn't seen what he has purchased? He's dumber than my cousin Otto. The third man perhaps has a sliver of an excuse—he has a new wife he must cheer up.

In the Sermon on the Mount, the condensed description of the lifestyle of the Christian, we are told not to worry, but to trust God, and to *seek the Kingdom of God first.* Folks, God expects us to get our priorities straight, and not to put off entering the Kingdom of God. On this matter of spiritual procrastination, this "putting off what we know we ought to do," the Bible says it is arrogant to assume we have many years left in which to make our spiritual decisions. You don't know how long you will live. Therefore do not procrastinate in spiritual decisions. On the other hand, it is sad to see how many people say they are Christians, but their long life has produced no evidence. They were always "going to get involved in the church"; always "going to obey God's teachings" but never did.

Don't procrastinate.

If You Know What's Good for You

In the morning service at the First Baptist Church in West Jefferson where I am presently serving as Interim Pastor we pass a "Friendship Pad" during the welcome part of the service. The members of the church sign at the bottom of the sheet, and the guests fill in the upper portion of the sheet, giving the pastor information about them and their needs. It's a helpful tool to build attendance, especially since I phone in this "roll call" every Monday morning to the Lord. —Just kidding! (Although some of my parishoners feel certain I am keeping roll). It is a good means to share prayer needs and get to know the guests in our midst.

But all kidding aside, apparently being in church on Sunday is one of the safest places you can be. According to one pollster, Mark Moring, we need to take steps to be safe in the world today. He suggests the following:

1. Avoid riding in automobiles because they are responsible for 20 percent of all fatal accidents. The other 80 percent probably includes such things as falling off the roof, etc.

2. Do not stay at home because 17 percent of all accidents occur in the home. Well, most of us aren't home much anyhow.

3. Avoid walking on streets or sidewalks because 14 percent of all accidents occur to pedestrians. Where would he have us walk? In the highway?

4. Avoid traveling by air, rail, or water because 16 percent of all accidents involve these forms of transportation. Yep, I took a neighbor fishing in my canoe the other day and he turned it over.

5. Of the remaining 33 percent, 32 percent of all deaths occur in hospitals. Apparently, above all else, we should avoid hospitals like the plague.

Well, Moring concludes by saying that you will be pleased to know that only .001 percent of all deaths occur in Sunday morning worship services, and these are usually related to previous physical disorders. So, logic tells us that the safest place to be at any point in time is at the church! Of course I still remember the time, while our church was telecast live each Sunday, that a church member had a cardiac event in the midst of the service, and several physicians went to his aid. The ambulance was called, and the medics brought in a stretcher and took him out of the service, none of which was seen by folks at home, because the television cameras stayed trained on the pulpit area. I figured it wouldn't help for the rest of us to crowd around the man anyway! He later was released from the hospital, none the worse for wear.

Yet, I rather like this man's way of thinking! Of course, when the Lord's ready for you, it doesn't make a lot of difference where you are or what you're doing. But, taking some precautions might keep you from booking the trip to glory on your own! So, the good word is this: If you know what's good for you, be in church Sunday. You'll be happier, and so will your pastor.

In the Grand Scheme of Things

A hundred years or so ago, when I was in elementary school, one of the customs that remain strong in my memory yet was the celebration of Confederate Memorial Day. On April 26 or a day close to it, the students were all taken down to the city cemetery, to decorate the 23 confederate graves there. All in a line, with a small raised concrete speaker's platform in the middle of the line, the gravestones were sacred. The speeches, the flowers, and the small confederate flags made a tremendous impression on young minds.

I grew up savoring that strong patriotism of a lost cause, the Confederacy. Those 23 soldiers had died in the great battle of Olustee, Florida. These 23 wounded men had been brought to the Smith Mansion, the only antebellum house in my home town of Madison, Florida, after the pivotal and bloody battle. At least I thought it was a pivotal and bloody battle.

For those few of you who may not have been aware of this awful battle, here are the salient facts. The Yankees had decided in early 1864 to invade Florida by way of Jacksonville and cut off the Confederate supplies from Florida, enlist blacks into the Union army, and set up a provisional state government. Union General Seymour had under his command about 5500 troops and 16 cannon, while the Confederate Generals Finegan and Colquitt had slightly less than that number under their command. The Union force moved from Jacksonville west through northern Florida, and some 50 miles or so from Jacksonville, at a place called Olustee or Ocean Pond, the two forces met on February 20, 1864. The battle took place in pine thickets and open ground, without any breastworks. By nightfall the Yankees had a bellyful and retreated toward Jacksonville. The battle casualties amounted to 1,861 Yankees and 946 Confederates. In terms of the percentage loss of the troops involved, while minor in numbers, it

Modern Parables   137

was one of the bloodiest battles of the War.

And yet, in the larger scheme of things, it was hardly worth mentioning—and isn't, in most books about the War. The years went by, the decorations were laid and speeches made annually, and I grew up. Yes, I grew up and forgot about Olustee. It seemed to me too, in my adult life, that my childhood visions of the greatness of Olustee and our little town's part in it were vastly overblown, in the grand scheme of things. And then, a dozen or so years ago, while on a leaf-peeping tour in New England, as I drove around the circle surrounding a statue in a little Massachusetts town, some writing on the monument caught my eye. I pulled over, got out and walked back to the monument. Yes! There it was, clearly stating that men from this town, in the 54th Massachusetts Infantry, had fought at the battle of Olustee!

In the grand scheme of things, that battle wasn't important. But to families in that little New England town, and to families in my hometown, and to the shaping of my childhood, it was very important. I got to thinking about this the other day, when I was given a book—a whole book, mind you—on the battle of Olustee. Perhaps those things which aren't important in the grand scheme of things in the world's view just may be important on some other level. Who's to say what is really important and what is not?

I suspect that when all is done, the really important things will be those that are important in the sight of God. Things like your helping that family in need, or the time you helped the older lady with her groceries, or the visits you made to the nursing home or hospital just to cheer up folks you didn't even know. I've decided that "the grand scheme of things" refers to the way God intends things to be, not the way the world judges events.

So, go do some deed of kindness. You may never see how important it is in the grand scheme of things, but do it anyway!

We Will Miss You, Charlie

It happened a dozen years ago while I was a pastor in Memphis. Our ministerial staff was tearing along the dark rural road, coming back one night from a staff planning retreat. As we sped through the night a patch of light appeared in the darkness—a lighted church steeple. We could see it over a couple of hills, and then we saw a vapor light or two, and realized we were coming into a village. Now we were racing toward the church, visible down the road. As we were about in front of the little rural church, two things struck me: first, the lighted sign in front of the church had this message: *We will miss you, Charlie.* And then, I glanced at the front door of the church as we sped by and saw through the open door a coffin down in front of the pulpit, banked by flowers on either side. It was Charlie. We had darted out of the darkness to see the lighted steeple and this scene, and just as quickly we were lost again in the darkness. All the rest of the way back to Memphis I pondered this scene. The message of the sign kept drumming in my head: *We will miss you, Charlie.* I wondered who Charlie was. I wondered about the message on the sign—clearly it wasn't for Charlie to read; perhaps for his family; perhaps for passersby like us? I wondered what kind of man Charlie was; what kind of work he did; whether he was a Christian.

I told my wife the story, and she suggested that maybe the church put up the sign whenever anyone in the community died. I thought about that. What if Charlie were the local bootlegger? For the church to say they would miss Charlie in that case would take more of the grace of God than most churches have! I don't know anything, really, about Charlie. But this I know, Charlie is the story of each one of us.

"We will miss you, Charlie." Charlie's gone, and so is JFK and Elvis and Dale Ernhardt and a host of others— every day—that we

didn't count on dying when they did. Charlie will no longer be found in his usual places during the day; at the close of the day; or on Sunday. Charlie's gone. The sign preaches eloquently a biblical truth we want to ignore: *we are all going to die someday, unless Jesus returns first.* If we are wise, we will contemplate the reality of our death. After all, only man, of all living creatures, knows he will die.

"We will miss you, Charlie." That bit of lighted sign raises the question, What was the point of Charlie's life? Why was he here? Why did Charlie live and die in that particular community? *Why are we here? What is the purpose of life?* Depending upon your view of life, Charlie's life was either a blind happenstance, random genes calling to genes, or the beautiful, intricate plan of Almighty God. If Charlie's life—and your life and mine—is the plan of God, than words like *purpose, meaning, fulfillment, hope, joy, peace* ought to be used to describe Charlie's life. Everybody wants those words; everybody wants a sense of fulfillment and purpose and joy and peace. The Bible tells us this is God's intention for our life. Jesus said, *"I came that they might have life, and have it more abundantly."* Did Charlie understand that God was his silent partner in blessings? Did Charlie understand that God knew all about him and still loved him? Did Charlie realize that rejection of God's forgiveness and shaping Spirit makes our lives empty and futile?

"We will miss you, Charlie." But notice that Charlie not only died, he is *missed.* Will you be missed when you're gone? Will it make any difference to anybody that you lived? I don't know what Charlie did in that community, but he left a hole, a gap, a tear in the fabric of the community when he left. Another way of putting this: Charlie's gone—what'd he leave behind? He's done whatever he's going to do in this world. And the newspaper no doubt spoke of those he left behind. But it didn't mention the most important thing he left behind—his *influence.* He had influence, you know. For good or bad. There are children whose lives were shaped by Charlie without his saying a word . . . just by the way he lived and what they saw. For in

each of our minds is a huge collection of memories of those people around us as we grew as children.

We will miss you, Charlie. Charlie's gone—where'd he go? Now there's a question for you. *Where did Charlie go?* Not even Joe, who never darkens the church door, believes that Charlie just *ended*; that Charlie doesn't exist anymore. Something in us says that this life is not the end. Polls show that an overwhelming majority of both churched and unchurched people believe in a hereafter. Of course, a lot more people believe in heaven than in hell. Remember the little jingle, *I had an old dog named Rover; when he died he died all over."* That may be true of dogs, but it's not true of people. Charlie's gone to either heaven or hell. And he has gone there not on the basis of his deeds, on the basis of whether he was a good man or a bad man. *Every one of us goes to heaven or hell based not on deeds, but on whether or not we trusted Jesus as our Lord and Saviour.* Remember the words of Jesus that most all of us learned as a little child: *"For God so loved the world, that He gave His only begotten Son, that whoever believes in Him should not perish, but have eternal life."*

We will miss you, Charlie. If Charlie was a Christian, his friends at that little church could have added: *only for a little while!* Until all God's children meet again in a land where there is no sickness, no sorrow, no sin, no death. Now that's something to think about.

Blundering Toward the Light

He said it was a terrifying moment. Something we who grew up in America cannot quite grasp. He's my neighbor, and he was telling me about his experience of coming to America after the Second World War. He was too young to be a soldier in Hitler's Germany, although his older brother was in the Hitler Youth. My neighbor, as an eight-year-old, broke his arm falling out of an abandoned German

fighter plane six days after the war ended. He and other kids were stealing the clocks from the planes at the airfield near his home.

Anyhow, he finished what we would call high school and college, and did his *practicum*, a sort of internship, at a company which was designing machinery for textile mills in America. Said he, "I was absolutely broke. It took half my salary for food, almost half for lodgings—I couldn't even ask a girl out on a date." That's enough to pray about, and one Friday he sat down and asked the Lord to intervene. He is a religious man, my neighbor, but not overmuch so. On Monday after his prayer, he says he got a call from the American Embassy, saying there was a visa and travel permit waiting for him at the Swiss Air counter. He knew nothing about it, and was told that a textile company in America was having trouble with their machinery, and upon contacting the manufacturer had been given his name as one who helped design the machinery!

So, off to America with him. His insecurity deepens when he realizes that Americans don't speak German, and he certainly doesn't speak English—not the kind you find outside restrooms, anyhow. He is met at the airport in New York by a man who speaks a smattering of Dutch, so they can communicate. They stop on the way to his destination to eat. His unease is racheted up several notches when his companion immediately orders a hamburger to eat—my friend is from the Hamburg area of Germany! (They eat people over here?) And then his companion adds to his confusion by ordering up some fried frenchmen!

He laughs about things like that nowadays. But he hasn't forgotten how he blundered toward the light of a deeper faith. He has done very well, with God's help, in America. And he hasn't forgotten how God hears prayers. He doesn't think all prayers are answered in three days, as his prayer was. But, he says, God does indeed answer prayers. Not always in material ways, but God is there, in the dark times as well as the sunshine, leading us.

We are into the Advent season, the time of the coming of the Messiah into this world, and I reflect on how the Jewish people were always blundering toward the light, the light of the world which is Christ. It's a zigzag route they took, from Abraham to Egypt, from slavery to idolatry, from rebellion to kingship, from tabernacle to temple, from true commitment to business-as-usual religion. Somehow their hardships and exiles didn't open their eyes; yet they were blundering toward the fulness of time. Blundering toward the everlasting light that still shines in the dark streets of hundreds of villages including Bethlehem.

I sometimes marvel at my neighbor's stumbling onto a deep and meaningful faith even in the midst of the horrors of a world war, as a child in the midst of the terrors of Nazi Germany even for Germans, in the midst of very hard times in the aftermath of that war. Yet he and his wife are active in and support several churches—yes, they are Lutheran—and he is one of the kindest men I know. And he stumbled into the light of Christ.

As the New Testament age opened, Jesus' own people, beat down and discouraged, stumbled not toward the light, but away from it. "He came unto his own, and his own received him not." So says the Gospel of John. In this season of Advent, when we think deeply about the coming of Christ, let us recover the deeper meaning of Advent, and search our hearts to see if we are ready, ourselves, to prepare him room.

When Earth's Last Picture Is Painted

I figured if Winston Churchill could take up oil painting in his retirement, why couldn't I? So I did. Well, that's not exactly true; I used to do what folks call "glass blowing"—watch those comments about preachers and hot air—but watching my wife break objects while

dusting, I decided that if I wanted to leave something for the grand-kids, I had better take up an unbreakable hobby! That was about 20 years ago, and I have found oil painting to be very rewarding. Even if only a mother could love some of my paintings! Then again, quite a few are in private collections of friends and others.

There are all kinds of painters and paintings. Some folks say that if they want a picture of a landscape, they'll just take a photo of it. These folks mistakenly think that a landscape artist is trying to be photographically correct. But the artist is trying to bring out on the canvas the special character of what he or she sees in that old tree, or that mountain scene or whatever. I guess it's kin to Michelangelo chipping away all the extra stone to get to the angel he sees beneath!

When I'm in a thoughtful mood and dabbling with my oil paints, I reflect that God is like an artist; he sees something special in each of us, and our lives are his painting—as far as we will let his brush have freedom. We who are artists are aware how we fail to draw forth the essential beauty and character of even an old stone. And when we try to paint portraits, we who are amateur can be laughable. I embarked upon a season of portrait painting about a year ago, and painted a recognizable portrait of three of my grandchildren, and a fair portrait of my wife. Then, emboldened with pride, I decided to paint a self-portrait. After all, Rembrandt was always painting himself, and Van Gogh chopped his ear off and then did a self-portrait. I didn't go that far, you understand. Well, when I finished the painting, I had to say that it was a quite good painting of a minister in his robe, holding the Word—just the sort of thing you might see hanging in a library or church parlor. I showed it to my wife with this comment: "I think its a quite good painting; if I ever run into the fellow I've painted, I'm going to give him this portrait!"

You see, while the painting was all right, I failed to catch what-ever it is that makes Earl Davis unique. And we are all unique, you know. My, how we gum that word "unique" to death! We hear TV talking heads speak of someone being "quite unique" or "mighty unique". The truth is, "unique" means that you are one of a kind. You cannot be halfway unique. Each of us is completely unique. Just as no two snowflakes are the same, no two persons are totally alike. It's just like God to make each of us special and different, filled with a delightful, unique character. What a God, and what a plan!

Well, I'd best get back to the painting I'm working on. Do you remember that poem of Rudyard Kipling:

When Earth's last picture is painted,
and the tubes are twisted and dried,
When the oldest colors have faded,
and the youngest critic has died,
We shall rest, and, faith, we shall need it
—lie down for an aeon or two,
Till the Master of All Good Workmen
shall put us to work anew.

And those that were good shall be happy:
they shall sit in a golden chair;
They shall splash at a ten-league canvas
with brushes of comets' hair;
They shall find real saints to draw from
—Magdalene, Peter, and Paul;
They shall work for an age at a sitting,
and never be tired at all!

And only the Master shall praise us,
and only the Master shall blame;
And no one shall work for money,
and no one shall work for fame;
But each for the joy of the working,
and each, in his separate star,
Shall draw the Thing as he sees It
for the God of Things as They are!

Yes, the best is yet to be.

Made in the USA
Columbia, SC
04 June 2022

61317651R10085